A CALL
TO
SHARE

*Frances,
My classmate
the greatest of the
great. I love you
Zen*

Zke Zimmerman

DORRANCE
PUBLISHING CO
EST. 1920
PITTSBURGH, PENNSYLVANIA 15238

Dorrance Publishing Co
585 Alpha Drive
Pittsburgh, PA 15238
Visit our website at *www.dorrancebookstore.com*

ISBN: 978-1-6853-7346-7
eISBN: 978-1-6853-7662-8

A CALL
TO
SHARE

TABLE OF CONTENT

INTRODUCTION

This book is a collection of letters that together define and identify systemic racism in America. Systemic racism, as argued here, is much more about acts of omission than acts of commission. The letters contained herein address systemic racism and how it's manifested in various segments of our society – education, corporate/business, government, and The Church – most frequently through acts of omission.

Those who do not understand racism and those who avoid understanding racism represent an important audience for this book. It is this demographic -- a large segment of the American society – whose worldview is most threatened by any acknowledgment of racism. This book explores details of that threat.

Each letter in this book contains suggested (admittedly often partial) solutions to the dominant manifestations of racism in a selected segment of our society (e.g. education, business, etc.). These solutions necessarily cut to the core of the setting being addressed, because systemic racism knows no bounds. The solutions offered generally require profound, quite possibly traumatic, changes. We have not reached our current state of systemic racism overnight. In the American society, for Minorities (particularly non-European), it is the accumulation of racist polices and lifestyles over the last 300 years. Consequently, solutions will often cut deep, requiring significant changes, and will take generations to rid American society of this scourge.

A CALL TO SHARE

For a while now, I have had this feeling of an obligation to share some thoughts on what's happening in our country. What's happening today is not solely due to the deaths of several Blacks within recent months. It is the result of over 300 years of history. For me personally, it's the result of what I have experienced over the last 65 years. This journey started for me when at the age of nine years old, the Klu Klux Klan drove into my neighborhood and burned a cross. I was brought up in the church, and to this day, I can't connect how burning a cross would be the action of a Christian. We would become very upset if someone burned an American flag, so it seems even more upsetting that someone would burn a cross - the symbol of Christ giving his life to save us all. Yet those who burned the cross declared themselves Christians (for many of them), and this was condoned by other "Christians." Condoned by remaining silent (omission).

At the age of 16, I had my second significant event. I was working for the school system delivering supplies between schools and the warehouse. I was taking new books and materials to the "White Schools" from the warehouse; picking up used books and materials from the White Schools and delivering them to the "Black Schools"; picking up old books and materials from the Black Schools and delivering them to the dump. In the process, two things surfaced: 1) the Black Schools were only getting used books and materials, and 2) the students at the White Schools did not pay a rental fee for use of the books and materials, while the students at the Black Schools paid a non-refundable rental fee for books and materials.

At that point, I joined the Civil Rights Movement of the '60s – protesting the inequities in our society as a result of race. At the time, I was not allowed (by law) to attend a "White University" (e.g., USC, UGA, Clemson, etc...). I could not get a job in any restaurant (except as a cook or dishwasher), department store, medical facility, bank, and the list goes on. The reason was the color of my skin. Was that right? If it weren't, why didn't Christians say something?

At the age of 20, I joined the military and served for 27 years. I served in Vietnam and was wounded in 1969. In 1970, as I was driving between duty stations in the U.S., I was stopped by a highway patrolman who started by saying, "Boy, get out of the car and put your hands up." I was not speeding and there was no other violation I had committed. I was driving a new car and I was a young Black man. Since that time to today, I have been stopped several times with similar results by the patrolmen or police officers. That is what is now referred to as "Driving While Black" (DWB).

There is no debate that much progress has been made since I started this journey; however, there are still many inequities in our society that keep us from being able to say we experience equality – as pronounced by the U.S. Constitution. You see, for many people who look like me, my success is an anomaly. It took much more than hard work. God provided many angels along the way to carry me through difficult times that most people who look like me can't survive. During the Civil Rights Movement (1963-1966), the Chief of Police was that angel who protected me. He arrested me numerous times personally to protect me from the brutality I would likely have experienced if his police officers (all White) had arrested me. In the military, I was very fortunate at the second lieutenant level, there was a White Colonel – Colonel Frank E. Burdett, who took me under his wings and carried me to heights that others like me were not permitted to go. However, going these places was the norm for the White officers.

Later in my military career, other angels were provided to protect me. I was carried by two generals who later served as Chief of Staff of the

Army – Generals Carl Vouno and Dennis Reimer. As I sat on multiple promotion boards, I was repeatedly coached by Black Generals that I had a vital mission. That mission was to protect Black officers who had performed well; however, they did not receive the ratings they should have because of prejudices. Every Black officer in the rank of Colonel and above understands that, because each has experienced it – without exception.

Once I retired from the military and moved into the civilian community, without fail within the real estate business we were guided or warned about "communities based on Race." Because of my experiences, we ignored the warnings; however, others who look like me often have no basis for going against the warnings.

Sunday morning is the most segregated time in America (Blacks attending "Black churches" and Whites attending "White churches." This is and has always been confusing to me. If we all worship the same God, why can't we worship together? When I was 17 years old, I was arrested for attempting to go worship at a White church. Throughout my military career, we worshiped with all who believed in Jesus Christ and believed that He died on the cross for our sins, and that he rose from the grave. We have continued that to this day. Church and worship have posed some questions that are long standing. As we define "conservatives" and "liberals," would Christ be considered a conservative or a liberal? If He would be considered a conservative, then what would the Sadducees and the Pharisees be?

There are some big issues which contribute significantly to the long-standing unrest the country is experiencing. Just imagine if these conditions were you:

1. In recent decades, rich Black kids have been more likely to go to prison or be shot by law enforcement than poor White kids.

2. Black males are twice as likely as White males to be portrayed as perpetrators and criminals, and four times more likely to have their mug-shots included in the lead story.

3. In the American Education System, people who look like me are not really included in the curriculum. White students get no understanding of Latinos or Latino culture, nor African Americans or African American culture.

4. The overestimation of a Black child's age begins as young as 6, impacting the way they are seen and treated by others. There are expectations on them that they are not mature enough to meet – often resulting in being placed in Special Education. (Note: this was a big issue with our son, Rodney)

5. Large or tall Black males are perceived as particularly dangerous and treated as a threat. Thus, more police stops. White males may benefit from height. It is not unusual for a Black person to be followed around in a store like he/she is being watched. This is particularly true in an upscale store or shop. (I am tall, and my son is tall – that has oftentimes been a liability).

6. The racial wealth gap between Black and White families in America grew by 50% in the last 25 years due in large part to the fact that Black wealth has remained stagnant, and in many cases, lost ground. "When White America gets a cold, Black America contracts pneumonia."

7. "The wealth gap in America....Whites have 13 times the net worth of Blacks, the largest wealth gap that's existed since 1989....Home ownership declined faster among minorities than Whites....Only 47.4% of minorities were homeowners...But 73.9% of Whites owned homes."

8. The "Role Model Affect:" One Black male teacher in elementary school led to an increased expression of interest in college by African American boys and increased the number of Black boys taking a college entrance exam by 10%. (Note: At the elementary school level, numerous schools with a large population of Black boys have no Black male teacher).

Many have applauded the work that I did with youth in the Savannah Area. I did nothing beyond what God has called all of us to do. I could not do enough to go above and beyond what God has called us to do. All

I could do – even when I did all I could – falls short of the mark set by God. My guilt - could I have done more? – never look what I've done. I could never do enough.

The irony is that God gave the mission to every Christian as Christ said to his disciples:

"All authority in Heaven and on Earth has been given to me. Go therefore and make disciples of all nations, baptizing them in the name of the Father and of the Son and of the Holy Spirit, teaching them to ob-serve all that I have commanded you. And behold, I am with you always, to the end of the age." *Matthew* 28: 18-20.

Thus, I ask all – all races, all genders, all ethnicities (ALL), to heed the words of our Savior. That means we cannot sit silently during this time. Doing nothing is the sin of Omission. This day, this time – the time of the coronavirus, the time of civil unrest – is God's time. "This is the day the Lord has made; we will rejoice and be glad in it." Psalm 118:24.

SECOND LETTER:
A CALL TO SHARE

First, thanks for your response. I have concluded there is no short answer to the challenges we are experiencing with race and racism. The situation has been building for over 490 years – longer than the Israelites being held in slavery in Babylon. The difference, of course, is the situation in America has changed over time. This has led some to think that racism has been eradicated.

Short history lesson: 1) "There were significant numbers who were brought in as early as 1526. That year, some of these enslaved Africans became part of a Spanish expedition to establish an outpost in what is now South Carolina," according to Linda Heywood, a professor of African History and the History of the African Diaspora and African American Studies at Boston University. 2) "*Christopher Columbus* likely transported the first Africans to the Americas in the late 1490s on his expeditions to Hispaniola, now part of the Dominican Republic. Their exact status, whether free or enslaved, remains disputed. But the timeline fits with what we know of the origins of the slave trade." (History.com) 3) Virginia colonist *John Rolfe* documented that, "In late August 1619, the *White Lion*, an English privateer commanded by John Jope, sailed into Point Comfort and dropped anchor in the James River." The arrival of the ship and "20 and odd" Africans on board is immortalized in textbooks, with 1619 often used as a reference point for teaching the origins of *slavery in America*."

Why is that little piece of history so important? Because since the beginning of slavery, different things have been handed down from generation to generation and that's still happening. Two examples: 1) Since the beginning of slavery, many have been taught that Blacks are inferior and Whites are superior. The Bible and science have frequently been used to justify that thesis. This has been often taught by Whites to their children and Blacks to their children. 2) Blacks have been portrayed and treated as sub-humans. This has been the practice in the past and still is in a number of different areas – e.g., Black men are stronger and thus to be feared physically. In order for an organization or team to be successful, there must be a White man in charge. Neither of these is the case 100% of the time; however, they do still exist and in sufficient frequency to have an impact.

One of the major factors in the solution set for eradicating racism is education coupled with sensitivity. A current example is President Trump scheduling a rally in Tulsa, Oklahoma for June 19th. Why is that a slap in the face? In many places, June 19th, also known as Juneteenth, is a big celebration recognizing the end of slavery in America.

After the Civil War came to a close in the spring of 1865, General Granger's arrival in Galveston that June signaled freedom for Texas's 250,000 slaves. Although emancipation didn't happen overnight for everyone—in some cases, slave owners withheld the information until after harvest season—celebrations broke out among newly freed black people, and Juneteenth was born. That December, slavery in America was formally abolished with the adoption of the *13th Amendment*.

The year following 1865, freedmen in Texas organized the first of what became the annual celebration of "Jubilee Day" on June 19. In 1979, Texas became the first state to make Juneteenth an official holiday. Today, 47 states *recognize* Juneteenth as a state holiday, while efforts to make it a national holiday have so far stalled in Congress.

It is a further slap in the face with the rally being held in Tulsa, Oklahoma. In the early 1900s, Tulsa's Black population was economically thriving. From 1905 to 1921, Greenwood – the Black community of Tulsa – grew to be known as the Black Wall Street. "In 1906, O.W. Gurley, a wealthy Black landowner, bought 40 acres of property in Tulsa and named it Greenwood after the Mississippi city. He started a boarding house for African Americans, ensured land was sold only to Black people and provided loans for new business ventures. Soon other Black entrepreneurs flocked to the area. J.B. Stradford started the country's largest Black-owned hotel. A.J. Smitherman, a publisher, founded the Tulsa Star, a Black newspaper. The district, population 10,000, became a bustling enclave of grocery stores, hotels, schools, churches, libraries, luxury shops, banks and two movie theaters. But the success of the area, which included both wealthy and middle-class residents, fueled jealousy, particularly among less fortunate whites." *Paul Davidson*, USA TODAY, 15 June 2020.

"In 1921, a white mob attacked a predominantly Black area in Tulsa, killing hundreds of people and destroying the country's wealthiest African American community. Its abrupt demise and similar incidents around the country during that period played a role in widening the racial wealth divide. The history of the massacre in the area, which was also known as 'Black Wall Street,' has shined a spotlight on the formation of an affluent Black community and the gruesome events that destroyed it." *Sources: History.com, Tulsa Historical Society and Museum, newspaper and other historical accounts and interviews.*

Although President Trump has changed the date to 20 June, that is still a negative action to dispelling the thoughts that his actions are a slap in the face to the people of Tulsa, Oklahoma who are trying to build a positive racial environment in their city.

This highlights the requirement that our leaders at all levels be educated and empathetic to Black History.

As more days go by and the protesting continues, I am more apprehensive about any real progress being made about the state of racism in America. When I was growing up, my dad always told us to walk in the other persons shoe before criticizing them. He was absolutely right. I don't see any evidence (on a large scale) of Whites understanding what it means when I say I have been stopped by the police numerous times when there was no offense. I don't know if others can grasp how a Black male has to fear for his life every time he leaves home. A young man was killed by the police in Atlanta last week as he ran away. Some will say, "Well, he shouldn't have run." That's true. But the bigger issue is – was that of the magnitude that he should be killed? When I was demonstrating in the '60s and dogs were sent to attack the demonstrators – was exercising my constitutional right countered by attack dogs the right thing? When George Floyd was killed for allegedly trying to pass a counterfeit $20 bill, was that of the magnitude to kill him?

When it is said "Black lives matter," the effort is to show for hundreds of years things have been done that send the message that Black lives don't matter. It is NOT saying other lives do not matter. It's like someone saying my father has cancer and the other person responding, "Oh a lot of people get sick." Or when your wife says, "Do you love me?" And you respond, "I love everybody." If you haven't tried that, try and see how she responds.

If anyone has trouble seeing how the President's rally in Tulsa on Saturday is a slap in the face to the Black community of Tulsa and in general, this is not a rally for those celebrating Juneteenth....Much to the contrary. .

THIRD LETTER:
A CALL TO SHARE

As the COVID Virus continues to impact our lives and as protests continue over racial inequities, many of voicing concerns and confusion.

I saw this shared by several people on FACEBOOK: *"I'm so confused right now. I see signs all over saying black lives matter. I'm just trying to figure out which black lives matter. It can't be the unborn black babies. They are destroyed without a second thought. It's not black cops. They don't seem to matter. It's not my black conservative friends. They are told to shut up if they know what's best for them by their black counterparts. It's not black business owners. Their property does not mean anything. It's not blacks who fought in the military. Their statues are destroyed by the black lives matter protesters with disdain. So, which black lives matter again?....I'm really confused now. Look at the data, NO, not that data. Do the math. No, you can't do the math like that. Only the experts can understand the data and math. What do you mean other cities/states/governors are interpreting the data differently? Pools are safe in Indiana, but not Michigan? Playgrounds are safe in your town but not mine? Amusement parks are safe in Florida, but not Ohio, nor Michigan.*

If you are silent, you are part of the problem. If you speak, you are part of the problem. If you have to ask, you don't understand. If you don't ask, you don't care.

For three months, NOTHING was more important than social distance. In fact, we gave up all of our liberties. In fact, we gave up all of our liberties for it. We canceled schools, medical and dental procedures, yet allowed the murder of babies, canceled activities, closed businesses, eliminated every spring rite of passage from prom to graduation, denied people funerals, even at Arlington, and we wrecked the economy for it. Then came social justice, and social distance was no more.

It's all so predictable, tedious, and exhausting. Nothing adds up. It's one gigantic math life problem, with ever changing denominators that I'm sure the media and politicians are eagerly ready to solve for us."

I can understand both the confusion and the concern.

Part I. *The Coronavirus.* Let's start with the virus. For Believers, we know that God is in charge - yes. We also know that we live in a sinful world. The virus has provided a stage for us to recognize our movement away from God. The virus brought a halt to all sports. We discovered that in many ways sports was becoming more and more of an idol god. An idol god is something that we place a higher priority on when the priority should be on God. The virus is an opportunity for us to recognize that and make changes in the direction we are going – direction back to the focus on God rather than sports.

The virus left millions of people unemployed. If we pay close attention, this highlights in many ways 1) the need for saving money, 2) for higher pay (especially for our emergency workers, police, firefighters, nurses and other medical personnel, and educators). Disney and other theme parks were close – cruise ships docked. Vacations were becoming more and more "a necessity" and costing thousands of dollars. The pandemic provided the opportunity for families to find different, less expensive ways to enjoy each other and have fun. 3) This has put a spotlight on how we should help each other. With millions not having food to put on their tables, many rose to the occasion to supply food banks, provide meals for emergency workers, and provide support as needed. When the farmers were going to have to throw away food because consumers didn't have money to purchase, we found ways to purchase the food and distribute it to food banks to be given to those in need. 4) The need for medical care for all has also been demonstrated. If medical care wasn't provided for all, then those who do not get medical care will infect those who can afford the medical care. For those opposed to "affordable health care," I hope the message is received that if we don't take care of all, then we all suffer.

Be thankful for the lessons we are being provided. We would be worse than the Isrealites if we don't heed the lessons.

Part II. *Black Lives Matter.* First and foremost, I restate that the theme "Black Lives Matter" is not at all implying that other's lives do not matter. It is about the dehumanized treatment received by Blacks from the time of being brought to America as slaves (1619) to today (2020). Hundreds were shackled and held in the lower sections of ships without food or drink and transported against their will, only to be sold into slavery when they arrived in "the home of the brave and the land of the free." Some would say, "That was hundreds of years ago, why are you still living in the past?" Well, the past has molded us into what we are today. My great-grandfather was a slave – was yours? My father was a sharecropper who was sent to jail by the landowner because my father tried to make money to support his family – was yours? I was arrested for attempting to attend church – were you? I was arrested for going to a restaurant to eat – were you? I was arrested for walking down the street with three other young Black men (none of whom had committed a crime) – were you? I was arrested 19 times and did not commit a crime any of those times – were you? Whenever a Black male is approaching, the average thought is that he is a "thug" or criminal. That has been preached since the 1950's and is still being preached today. For those of you who know me, know that I am no different than at least half of the Black men locked up in prison today. I am where I am and not where they are because of a few people (Christians) who had the faith to recognize that I was a human being and not a thug and to treat me like a human being. You see, Chief Harold Hall in Orangeburg, South Carolina went against those around him by treating me like a human being. He would not let the dogs attack us or let water hoses be used against us; each time he put me into his police car (12 times), he treated me with respect – like you would expect a Christian adult to treat a teenager. He knew that his other police officers were not likely to be that way. Chief Hall understood in 1963 that Black Lives Matter.

The theme, "Black Lives Matter," is saying, when all people are treated as their lives matter – then we can expect to move forward. Right now, that is not happening.

FOURTH LETTER:
A CALL TO SHARE

LIBERAL VS CONSERVATIVE

Before beginning a discussion on these terms, I have learned it is best to review the definition of each term.

Dictionary.com defines conservative as: "Disposed to preserve existing conditions, institutions, etc., or to restore traditional ones, and to limit change."

D*ictionary.com* defines *liberal as*: "Favorable to progress or reform, as in political or religious affairs. Favorable to or in accord with concepts of maximum individual freedom possible, especially as guaranteed by law and secured by governmental protection of civil liberties. Favoring or permitting freedom of action, especially with respect to matters of personal belief or expression: a liberal policy toward dissident artists and writers. Free from prejudice or bigotry; tolerant: a liberal attitude toward foreigners."

Now that we have the definitions before us, I think it would be fair to say that often times when these terms are used, it is not as defined above. When I hear the terms "liberal" and "conservative" used by Southern Whites, I get very confused. The term "liberal" when used in their presence, brought with it the implication that this is the epitome of profane language or insult. In fact, it carried the tone that one would prefer to be called any profane word before being called a "liberal." Going on the definition however, I thought it would be a good thing to be a person who is in favor of progress, and in favor of everyone being free from prejudice, bigotry and injustice. But, by that definition, that makes me a liberal.

It appears that these words have taken on some regional definitions. As a result, whenever it is used by two or more people who are not from the same general background and region, the terms are offensive and misinterpreted.

The term, conservative (the favored label), is one who favors tradition and generally suspect things that fall outside traditional views of "normal." For some from the South, tradition equates to the era of the 50's – the time before the Civil Rights Era of the '60's.

Rev. Dr. Joanna Adams, a retired pastor in the Presbyterian Church (USA) and has served as a trustee for the Presbyterian Church Foundation, Agnes Scott College and Columbia Theological Seminary, gave a description of her experience in the South in the 1950's. She provides many descriptors of what those good days were like. She wrote, "Southern is what I am through and through. I am also as White as a White person can be. When I traced my genealogy, I discovered that every single one of my ancestors many centuries back was from the British Isles, with a couple of Germans thrown in for diversity's sake. I am aware that all of us homo sapiens *can trace our beginnings to Africa*, but most White people couldn't care less.

As a child growing up in Mississippi in the 1950s, I thought nothing about race. I knew no Black people, other than the janitor at my school and our maid, Omera, whom I loved, but whose last name I never knew. My parents probably didn't either. They paid her in cash – I'm pretty sure it was not much. Occasionally, my mother did send her home with used tin cans full of bacon drippings.

One day, Omera told my mother that she and her family were moving to Detroit. It sounded like Mars to me. I cried. Omera and I hugged as we said goodbye. As we watched her walk to the bus stop down the street, Mother turned me around and said, "Jo, I know you love Omera, but I don't want you ever again to hug a Negra. It's just not done."

This was Mississippi in the 1950s. My father worked for the Chamber of Commerce in our town, Meridian. The big event of the year, both for the Chamber and for the city, was the Calf Scramble Parade on a spring Saturday. The preceding Friday night, our high school stadium would be filled with people from all over the county who had come to watch young men wrestle calves to the ground on the football field and lasso them. The victors would take their newly subdued calves to raise them, though eventually the calves would become cows and sold to a slaughterhouse.

Come Saturday, the city was gathered on downtown sidewalks for the best parade of the year: Men wearing ten-gallon hats and embroidered boots, riding on prancing stallions, bright red fire engines sounding their sirens, and the mayor sitting on the back seat of his convertible, his starched white shirt soaked with perspiration while he waved listlessly to the crowd.

Then came the floats, the skirts of which consisted of chicken wire, each little quadrangle of which was stuffed with white Kleenex bouquets, meant to look like carnations.

Lovely White girls sat on the floats, waving enthusiastically and smiling like Miss America. I wanted to be just like them. I was just a kid then, standing on the sidewalk with a couple of friends. We had ridden the bus downtown for a nickel. Ten or 11 years old, we were. Safe as could be. Besides, my father was in charge of the parade.

Then, this: A float from the Black grammar school in "colored town" came into view. I had never heard of that school and did not even know there was a Black grammar school.

But there was the float. Same chicken wire. Same Kleenex carnations. Riding on the float were three little girls looking like a million dollars in their ruffled dresses. The girls on the float were about my age, smiling with pride and delight.

All of a sudden, three White boys, much older than my friends and me, standing next to us in jeans, cowboy hats, and boots, yelled out, "No n——— wanted here." One of them walked toward the float and spit on one of the girls. Another, then another did the same. And so it went.

Looking closely at what Dr. Adams wrote, a few generalities can be gleaned about that era: 1) economically, white families were stable – that is there were primarily two economic classes – white collar and blue collar; 2) white communities were deemed very safe; 3) white children were very mannerly (when they were in the presence of adults); 4) whites had very little contact with blacks – primary contact was with housekeepers, janitors, and other lower labor categories; 5) white children had little to no contact with black children – their contact with blacks was as describe by Dr. Adams; 6) Jim Crow laws kept blacks from interacting with whites outside of the above described environments – they could not attend the same schools; they didn't go to church together (and generally still don't in 2020); they could not use the same restroom facilities in any public location; and they didn't use the same waiting rooms at doctors' offices, nor hospitals.

Question: Did you ever hear or know about Jim Crow laws when you were a child? Black children had to be keenly aware of Jim Crow laws because their lives depended on knowing and abiding by them. Examples: 1) a black person walking down the street – in many locations – had to move off the sidewalk when approaching a group of whites; 2) in public facilities, blacks had to use the facilities marked "colored" –those facilities were always substandard; 3) a black man or black boy could be arrested/beaten/lynched for looking at a white woman. An example of this treatment as given in Wikipedia, "Emmett Louis Till (July 25, 1941 – August 28, 1955) was a 14-year-old African American who was lynched in Mississippi in 1955, after being accused of offending a white woman in her family's grocery store. The brutality of his murder and the fact that his killers were acquitted drew attention to the long history of violent persecution of African Americans in the United States."

The term, conservative, carries a meaning for a culture. In *Southern Conservatives Are America's Third Party*, "The Southern conservative finds freedom and equality through adherence to a social hierarchy based on race, Christianity, a male duty to protect women, and a commodity driven economy….If a perfect society is formed in terms of culture, race, and religion, there is no such thing as "progress" (liberalism)." Thus, for many, that perfect (near perfect) society was in the 1950's.

This is not to imply that every person whose livelihood hinges on "conservativism" embraces the above paragraph. It does say that the "conservative ideology" is rooted in these principles – whether it is acknowledged or not. Ladd continues, "Thus freedom takes on a dependence on a racial, religious, and economic caste system that in order to maintain freedom/security, the lower order is described as dangerous and must be suppressed." The lower order here refers to the "have nots" – minority race, different religion and low economic holdings.

Hopefully, this letter provides some basis for thinking outside of whatever our past thought pattern has been with reference to these two concepts – conservative vs. liberal.

While the 1950's may have been GREAT days for some, they were NOT for ANY black person. Although Jim Crow laws have been eradicated in the formal sense, in many pockets of our society those same principles which led to the Jim Crow laws are still manifested in many of the culture's practices. Black boys and men still must be taught many of the things that existed under Jim Crow – known as "The Talk."

FIFTH LETTER:
A CALL TO SHARE

INDEPENDENCE DAY

We have just completed celebrating Independence Day, the 4th of July. Yes, I celebrated, like all Americans did and should. I am an American and I love this country. I have served our country through military service for 27 years. Because I served does not make me any more or less patriotic than those who didn't have the opportunity to serve.

That thought brings me to – what about those who had the opportunity to serve and avoided serving? When I was a teenager – during the sixties – the United States had a draft system in place for selecting young men to serve. The draft was there to fulfill the needs of the services when the needs were not met by volunteers. What is worthy of note here is that many of the same leaders of our nation who are now in their 70s avoided the draft. They used numerous techniques to avoid serving OUR country. Those whose parents were either in high places or had connections avoided the draft by getting deferments or joining the reserves or National Guard. Consequently, the ones who had no such connections were drafted. The irony of this entire process is that the ones who are now in their 70s and didn't serve are the very ones who are leading us and waving the flags and taking the platforms about being so patriotic. That appears to fall in the category of being a hypocrite.

Webster defines hypocritical as: characterized by behavior that contradicts what one claims to believe or feel: characterized by *hypocrisy*. *Also*: being a person who acts in contradiction to his or her stated beliefs or feelings: being a *hypocrite*. Synonyms include: artificial, backhanded, counterfeit, double-dealing, double-faced, fake, feigned, insincere, and Janus-faced.

My celebrating Independence Day is about this country – not about individuals. America is a great country with great ideals. It is with hope and faith that these ideals can and will be fulfilled one day.

As Americans, we celebrate the 4th of July as our Independence Day. I have a very close friend who is British and lives in the U.S. who does not celebrate the 4th with the same energy that we do; however, he respects our celebration. Personally, I don't get rattled by that. He is not an American. I have the utmost respect for the celebration of *Cinco de Mayo* on May 5th. However, I do not celebrate the same as those of Mexican or Hispanic descent. I and many others celebrate Juneteenth because of our origin. That does not make me any more or less American than another American of different origin. Unfortunately, there are some who do feel that those who celebrate Cinco de Mayo or Juneteenth are less patriotic or less American than they. It is the epitome of insult for one who claims to be patriotic to say to other Americans that they should "go back to where they came from." The only ones who might be positioned to make such a statement are the Native Americans.

The persons making statements such as those above are revealing character traits that are divisive to the country. These statements coupled with other actions of tweeting segments proclaiming "white power" and other ethnic slurs cannot and should not be ignored. To do these things and follow with an apology only magnifies the character of the individual. If it were said in the first place, that's the indicator of where the "Heart" is. There is a saying, "But the things that come out of a person's mouth come from the heart, and these defile them."

I have observed some inconsistencies in how we sometimes use generalities. For example, some police officers have killed unarmed Black men/kids and we say most police are good and we strongly support the police. And, in fact, I agree with that statement. Where the disconnect comes is when a police officer is killed, we say those protesters are violent and they should all be taken off the street. And what makes it worst is when our national leaders make the same type of generalizations. That has been the case for centuries. Consequently, when a Black person does some wrong deed, the generality follows that Black people do. The same type generalities tend to be made about most non-White ethnicities. For example, as the mass of immigrants were coming to the US from Central and South America, we repeatedly heard that they (all) were rapists, murderers, gangsters, etc. The majority of these immigrants were not in those categories; however, a negative label was put on all to give the impression they all were bad people. When the church massacre took place in Charleston, no one said or implied that white men are mass killers. Blacks and other minority groups have suffered throughout history with those type of negative generalizations. Oh, by the way, studies have shown that the average initial thought when one sees a Black male teen, their mind most often goes to 'he's a thug.' This contributes to many of the outcomes involving Blacks and other minorities.

I just saw where the President of the United States demanded that the Black NASCAR driver apologize for the "hoax" of having a noose in his car stall area. The FBI and others found that the rope was placed there years before. Therefore, the driver did not put it there and make up a story about it being placed there. As the administrator in high school for 22 years, one of the worse things I could have done was accuse a student who was being bullied that she/he was making this up. For an administrator/building leader to do something like that is unforgivable. But here, the top leader of the country does it. In many circles, that would be deemed sinful. How would you feel if your child came to you and said, "The principal called me a liar – that I was making it up?"

I recently read comments that there is no such thing as "White Privilege." Well, the narrative above is an example of White Privilege. I invite anyone who feels there is no such thing as White Privilege to have a discussion with practically any minority and you will receive numerous examples and situations where the outcome is determined or influenced by the race(s) of the persons involved.

White privilege is defined as the societal privilege that benefits white people over non-white people in some societies, particularly if all groups are otherwise under the same social, political, or economic circumstances. White privilege doesn't mean you don't have any hurdles, it just means you have fewer of them.

I will share from my experiences for your consideration situations of White Privilege: 1) As a teen, whenever I walked around in a department store such as Sears or JC Penney, it would not be very long before a sales person or security person would be following or keeping an eye on me; 2) When I purchased a new car, I was stopped multiple times and questioned when there was no traffic violation; 3) As a military officer for 27 years, it was always assumed that I was an enlisted soldier rather than an officer. On many of these occasions, a white person would be with me, and they were not labeled as enlisted.

Some other examples of White Privilege: 1) Do you have to inform your children of the harsh realities of systemic racism? 2) Do you know what it feels like to see your teenage son's death being mocked? 3) Do you have to worry about becoming the victim of law enforcement officers? 4) Do you know what it's like to have the following statistic looming over your head – one out of every four males of your race will go to jail at least once in his lifetime? 5) Do you have to constantly be aware that your clothing will label you as a thug, low-life, or gangster? 6) White privilege allows you to speak on any particular subject without being the sole representative for your entire race. 7) White privilege means no one questions why you got that really great job; it's assumed you were just highly qualified. 8) White privilege means not having to worry about your hair, skin color, or cultural accessories as the reason you didn't get a job. 9) White privilege means not having to worry about being stopped and frisked. 10) If you benefit from white privilege, you'll never be told to "get over slavery." 11) I Have The Privilege Of Learning About My Race In School (history books in school do not tell the Black story). 12) When you go to a job with an affirmative action employer do you have your co-workers on the job suspect that you got the job because of your race? 13)

Can you choose public accommodations without fearing that people of your race cannot get in or will be mistreated in the places you have chosen? 14) Can you travel alone or with your spouse without expecting embarrassment or hostility from those who deal with you?

This list may appear inconsequential to one who has never experienced these things. However, for many minorities (especially Blacks), these are not occasional encounters. Rather, these are as common as brushing your teeth. There is hardly a day that goes by without having multiple items of the above list come across the path of each Black person.

It is written that you must know that many will come claiming and proclaiming that they are righteous. The way to identify the righteous is NOT by their words, but rather by their deeds and their actions. When they do good deeds and brag about it, beware. It is written that we should not do things for notoriety. When a good deed is done for notoriety, it DOES NOT come from the heart. One who constantly brags and proclaims him/herself great appears to fit the description of one we should be weary of. However, in our society, oftentimes we are very attracted to the one who brags and claims his/her own greatness.

I would ask that if anything in this letter is contrary to what you believe, please email or call and let's talk about it. I understand that I don't see the world as everyone else does. This is not an attempt to get everyone to think like me. It is an effort to share what life is like for many and may be totally different from your experiences.

SIXTH LETTER: A CALL TO SHARE

RACIST VS RACISM (PT..1)

In 1992, I was stationed at Fort Leavenworth, Kansas, serving as the Chief of the Center for Army Leadership. While in that position, on one occasion I was briefing the top General in the British Army on American Military Leadership. His question to me during that briefing was, "Are the US Army's leadership principles based on Judeo-Christian principles/beliefs?" That was an easy question for me to answer. My response was, "Yes, they are." Two days ago, I heard another question, "Is the US operating on a foundation of 'White Supremacy?' That too was an easy question for me to answer. My response was, "Yes, it is." I will address that response more in subsequent letters. However, as we proceed, I needed to plant that seed early because in every area of our culture and society we want to examine if "White Supremacy" is a foundational issue.

Dictionary.com defines racism as: 1) a belief or doctrine that inherent differences among the various human racial groups determine cultural or individual achievement, usually involving the idea that one's own race is superior and has the right to dominate others or that a particular racial group is inferior to the others; 2) prejudice, discrimination, or antagonism directed against a person or people on the basis of their membership in a particular racial or ethnic group, typically one that is a minority or marginalized

Dictionary.com defines racist as: A label given to a person, or group of people who hate or dislike those who belong to a different race, believing that other races are not as good as their own and therefore treating them unfairly.

From these definitions, one can see that racism can be practiced by a person, persons, group, or culture without being racist. Terms are very important. An example of the importance of the meaning of a term is a Georgia State Senator who said the Black Lives Matter movement is a political statement. Well, that led me to find the definition of political statement. As defined on *www.definitions.net*, "The term political statement is used to refer to any act or non-verbal form of communication that is intended to influence a decision to be made for or by a political party." Using that definition to describe the Black Lives Matter movement totally misses the mark on describing it. The Black Lives Matter movement has absolutely NO political party association. The thought of aligning it with a political party, in and of itself, is divisive and deceitful. If it is not an intentional deceptive act, that means the person making the statement is operating from a base of ignorance. I am not sure which is the case; however, neither is acceptable from a leader – a Senator. To the contrary of being aligned with a political party, the Black Lives Matter movement is about equity, equality, fairness, economics, social, education, employment, religion, and practically any other category, but not political. This is a moral issue and has absolutely does not focus on aiding or supporting a political party.

Please allow me to share a very recent situation of the impact of being Black. One of my former students/mentees recently within the last 2 years graduated from the University of Georgia. He majored in finance and was a very good student – both in high school and college. He is now employed by a firm that pays its employees very well. This young man's starting salary is $80,000/year. That is great – right? Well, he is one of two Blacks of over 100 employees working at the level that he is. So far so good. Prior to the current year when there were no Blacks working there, the company had no outward recognition of Black History Month. This year, the two Black employees were tasked with planning and executing Black History Month recognition activities for the company. There are a few things wrong with this picture: 1) The planning and execution of these activities are separate from these two employees' primary function in the company. While they are planning and executing these non-mission functions, their White peers are moving out on mission functions. 2) This task is given to two neophyte employees who haven't been with the company long enough to know or understand what the true racial climate is within the company. Whatever activities they plan and execute will label them among all the employees in the company. This label oftentimes overshadows the performance or abilities these two have on mission related functions of the company.

This is not a unique situation I have just described. In 1973, the US Army established the Equal Opportunity Program. Officers and Senior Non-Commissioned officers were assigned as Equal Opportunity Officers and Equal Opportunity NCOs, respectively. High performing minority officers (primarily Black Captains) were assigned to organizations as the Equal Opportunity (EO) Officers. These officers were taken from the mainstream of their careers and placed in a basically non-career field. As a result of these assignments, when it was time for these officers to be considered for promotion, they were not competitive with other officers who remained in their career field. For example, a minority captain whose career field was Infantry and assigned as an EO Officer missed some key assignments in the Infantry career field (e.g., company commander, operations officer, instructor, et.al...). Thus, when it was time to be promoted to the rank of major (although he may have performed well as an EO Officer), he was not competitive with his peers in the Infantry career field. Therefore, he either left the military voluntarily or was forced out by being passed over for promotion.

I was given orders to be an EO Officer. However, I foresaw what would happen with my promotion opportunity. I told my assignments officer that I would not take that assignment. I was then given a direct order by him that I would take that assignment. I then took leave from my organization to travel to Washington, DC at my own expense to fight that assignment. I had a meeting with my assignment officer's boss – a colonel (I was a captain at the time). He told me the same thing – that I would take that assignment. I then arranged to talk with his boss – a brigadier general. After my conversation with him, I was no longer on orders to be an EO Officer. Very, very few Black Officers, if any, during the 70s served as EO officers and went on to achieve the rank of Colonel and none achieved the rank of General.

In corporate America, the field of education, and other professional sectors of our society, this is a form of systemic racism that is pervasive and keeps a significant percentage of Blacks and other minorities from moving to the executive level.

The common thread between the example of the Army EO program and corporate America is that leaders of organizations are seen as fully qualified to lead with no understanding or experience with people of color. A part of the reason that is the case is because our foundational norm is based on being White. That way of thinking forms a habit. The habit is that everyone and everything is measured on a "White" scale (e.g., role of mother, financial needs, behavior, and the list goes on and on). I share a quote from Robin DiAngelo in her book – *"White Fragility"* – on racism, "We (White people) must be willing to consider that unless we have devoted intentional and ongoing study, our opinions are necessarily uninformed, even ignorant… nothing in mainstream US culture gives us the information we need to have the nuanced understanding of arguably the most complex and enduring social dynamic (racism) of the last several hundred years."

Racism in an organization is a leadership issue. It is often viewed, however, as not germane to the main mission of the organization. Thus, it is not a "Board Room" issue. And since it is not a "Board Room" issue, it is not a major item or area to be dealt with individually or collectively. By "Board Room" issue, I mean it is not an issue which is used on the charts to show how well the company is doing.

SEVENTH LETTER: A CALL TO SHARE

RACIST VS. RACISM (PT..2)

What will it take to get Saul to understand that as much as he thought he was doing the right thing – he was not. Saul was very entrenched in his beliefs. Why was that and how did this come about? The modern-day Christian may see Saul as just an evil person. Phillip Long in his dissertation in 2012 points out, "One problem for modern readers is a misunderstanding about what Saul was doing. We tend to read modern persecution of Christians into the passage, or maybe lurid scenes from old movies of Nero throwing the saints to the lions. Nor should we think of rabbi Saul like a Puritan going door-to-door to root out the heretics. Stephen was teaching Jesus was the messiah, and in some way replaces worship in the Temple."

The critical point for Saul being the persecutor that he was possibly came when he attended the trial of Stephen. You see, Stephen was tried and killed for preaching that Jesus was the Messiah. It is believed that Saul was a high official who condoned the actions and possibly participated in the stoning of Stephen. The Saul-of-Tarsus.html also recorded, "… a trial that resulted in Stephen becoming the first Christian martyr. … Stephen's executioners laid their garments at the feet of Saul, who was in full approval of the mob's murderous actions. Saul later ravaged the church, entering the homes of believers and committing them to prison. Saul's anti-Christian zeal motivated him not only to arrest and imprison male Christians (the "ringleaders"), but to lock up female believers as well." As pointed out in Galatians 1:14, Paul states in regard to his actions as Saul, "I was advancing in Judaism beyond many of my own age among my people and was extremely zealous for the traditions of my fathers."

A search on the Life of Saul, www.gotquestions.org/Saul-of-Tarsus.html, reveals, "Saul of Tarsus was born in approximately AD 5 in the city of Tarsus in Cilicia (in modern-day Turkey). He was born to Jewish parents who possessed Roman citizenship, a coveted privilege that their son would also possess. Sometime between AD 15—20, Saul began his studies of the Hebrew Scriptures in the city of Jerusalem. It was under Gamaliel that Saul would begin an in-depth study of the Law with the famous rabbi."

Saul was seeing the world through his ancestors' eyes and not through God's eyes. That all changed as he was on the road to Damascus. As the story goes, Saul had a conversion experience. He was blinded, and once he began to see things God's way, he regained his sight.

There are a few points to be made from this segment of the transformation from Saul to Paul. The first is an examination of my beliefs. That's not easy. The beliefs of our ancestors are sometimes so woven into our belief system that we find it nearly impossible to see that some of our beliefs are not of God.

Some will teach – when a problem becomes too complex, begin your analysis with the basics. What are some of those basics: 1) Matthew 22:36-42, *36* "Teacher, which is the greatest commandment in the Law?" *37* Jesus replied: " 'Love the Lord your God with all your heart and with all your soul and with all your mind.' *38* This is the first and greatest commandment. *39* And the second is like it: 'Love your neighbor as yourself.' *40* All the Law and the Prophets hang on these two commandments." 2) John 3:17, "*17* For God did not send his Son into the world to condemn the world, but to save the world through him." 3) Micah 6:8, "He has shown you, O mortal, what is good. And what does the LORD require of you? To act justly and to love mercy and to walk humbly with your God."

I do not claim for a moment to be a Bible scholar nor theologian; I am just a person who has experienced the presence and power of God multiple times in my life. You don't have to be a Christian to recognize the value of the lessons available to everyone that are found in the Bible. For those reasons, this letter applies to everyone.

The connection begins with lessons about Paul and how they relate to the COVID-19 pandemic and the social unrest. The connection starts with recognizing that when a traumatic event happens, the lives of those affected by the event will never return to the way they were. So, it is with the pandemic and the social unrest, everyone affected by either will never have their lives return to the way it was before the epidemic. It is also important to look at the connections between the epidemic and the social unrest. Let there be no doubt, they are connected – if no more than by the effect that each has on the other.

The pandemic accentuates the impact being poor has on an individual, a family, and a community. When the pandemic hit and businesses, schools, restaurants, hotels, and many others had to close, the poor had no reserves available to them. They had no savings, no 401K to draw from, and no family that was in a position to take care of them until the economy returned to a state that they could return to work. Those who did not lose their jobs found that they had no option but to go to work – oftentimes exposing themselves to a higher level of risk. I submit that these circumstances are major contributors to the higher percentages of minorities contracting the virus and dying.

Another connection is the availability of healthcare, healthy lifestyle, and preventative medicine. Of course, those who can afford to have good health insurance plans are able to get regular checkups and medical care for minor illnesses. The poor fall short in these categories. Let me point out that poor is not limited to Blacks only – this is true for poor regardless of ethnicity. This is where the history is important. Blacks have a higher percentage among the poor in large part because of the plight of Blacks. One of the major areas when discussing the plight of Blacks is education.

A brief overview of the history of education for Blacks in America. During the slave era, a slave would be hung or severely beaten if it were discovered that he or she was learning to read. There was no formal education for slaves. After the slave era, there continued to be major efforts to keep Blacks from getting an education. It can be debated why that was the case; however, regardless of what one's debate premise(s) is, the fact remains that major efforts were put forth to keep Blacks from getting an education. After the formal end of slavery in 1865, as pointed out by Kate Kelly in *America Comes Alive (September 2015)*, "The Rosenwald Schools were built in the early 20th century as a solution to the scarcity of schools for African Americans in the rural south at that time. The school-building program was the idea of educator Booker T. Washington (1856-1915) who approached Julius Rosenwald, (1862-1932), the president of Sears, Roebuck and Company."

Prior to the Rosenwald Schools, there were some (not many) schools for African Americans opened in the northern states as early as 1752 in Philadelphia and 1787 in New York. While some free African Americans attended predominantly white colleges in the North during the antebellum era, educational opportunities in the south were rare. A Quaker philanthropist, Richard Humphreys, founded the nation's first black college, the Institute for Colored Youth in Philadelphia, in 1837. (*www.theclassroom.com/first-African American*.) Of course, in the south, the Jim Crow laws continued to prevent and marginalize the education for African Americans after slavery – segregated schools.

Labor intensive jobs were the vast majority (in many cases – only) of jobs available to Blacks from post-slavery through the 1960s. It was a "catch-22." A Black man could not get a good paying job because he didn't have the education. He couldn't get the education because there were few opportunities to do so. The low wages made it very difficult to get an education and subsist. This cycle continues today – 2020. The pandemic has highlighted this issue because with the closure of schools and resorting to virtual education/classrooms shows that a significant number of students do not have access to computers and other technologies.

Low wages, inadequate healthcare, and the high costs of education are major contributors to the social unrest. Certainly, the death of several

Blacks triggered the protest and provided a platform for protest. Also, I need to add that the lack of legal actions taken against those who caused the deaths is the critical feature. I submit however, that the above factors are the things that sustain the protests.

It's almost like it was yesterday that I remember being on the farm as sharecroppers. You see, my dad graduated cum laude from the second grade and my mother finished the third grade. But by the grace of God things happened in my family's life that caused us to not remain on the path of others from the area we were. For me, the course of my life changed when a lady – who later became my mother-in-law – took me to school with her when I was four years old. She was a teacher, and at the end of the school year, I was promoted to second grade. Because of false claims by the landowner about my family owing money, we had to flee from the farm. Ultimately, we wound up moving into a moderately sized town – Orangeburg, South Carolina. My father got a job as a janitor with the school system. Shortly after that, he became the custodian at one of the larger White churches in town. As the custodian at a church that had a school connected to it, he got much of the leftover food. That helped our grocery bill tremendously.

If we had to live solely from my father's salary, it's hard to predict what our outcome would have been. If any of the children had gotten ill, I don't know how we would have made it. As a family, we are very thankful for God's grace and God's mercy. Not all are as fortunate – in fact, most are not as fortunate. Most don't have any means of supplementing their low income. They don't have the good fortune not to get ill. They don't have the good fortune of others helping – as my first-grade teacher, Mrs. Smith, did. Others provided like help with my sister(s) and brother. Again, without it, I don't know what our family's story would be.

Now back to Paul and the Damascus Road. After his experience, he saw life through a totally different set of lenses than he did before the Damascus Road experience. So what lenses will we see through on our Damascus Road (the pandemic and social unrest)? Will we redistribute wealth? Will we increase wages in the low paying jobs? Will we have a mechanism to provide healthcare for those who can't afford it currently? Will we insure all students have the technologies necessary to get the same education as others during this time of school closures? Will we make colleges affordable?

In Paul's Damascus Road experience, he was blinded and would have his sight restored WHEN HE GOT HIS HEART RIGHT (WITH GOD) TOWARD ALL PEOPLE. WHAT WILL BE OUR FATE? Paul's life change was beyond what those who knew him would ever have imagined. Will ours be beyond what others who know us could ever imagine; or, will we work to keep things as they are? We are being provided a Damascus Road Experience. We must decide if we are to remain blind or if we shall see. God gives us choices. The choice is ours.

EIGHTH LETTER:
A CALL TO SHARE

WHY IT'S SO HARD TO GET TO EQUALITY

On Friday, 17 July 2020, two very prominent Civil Rights "Freedom Fighters" died. Friday morning, Reverend C.T. Vivian passed – he was known as Rev. Dr. Martin Luther King Jr.'s Field General. Friday evening, Congressman John Lewis passed – he was the youngest keynote speaker at the March on Washington in 1963. Both of these men were more than Civil Rights icons; they were "Freedom Fighters." Among those engaged in the lifelong fight for civil rights, a freedom fighter is one who is on the frontlines in the struggle.

As the news media was chronicling the lives of each of these men, it was evident that they were repeatedly fighting for the same thing. They fought for equality in voting and each time they fought the battle and won, somehow the results of each fight would be erased, and the battle would have to be fought again and again.

This letter is dedicated to the freedom fighters and illustrating how a country that claims to be the "Land of the Free and Home of the Brave" fights so vigorously to keep a segment of its population from being free. The timeline of events cited herein are taken from the Library of Congress document entitled: *The Civil Rights Act of 1964: A Long Struggle for Freedom: Legal Timeline, 2014*. Hopefully you will gain a better appreciation for the number of setbacks/roadblocks placed in the path of the fight for equality. Oh, by the way, according to the Constitution and numerous other Legislative documents, this fight for equality should not have been required. Not only was it required, but to date, the efforts are ongoing to take away victories that have been fought for multiple times. A prevailing example is the administration's efforts to repeal the Voter Rights Act of 1965 – a battle which has been fought over and over. I ask myself over and over, why is it so hard for everyone who professes to favor equality to see how hard the US Government works to keep segments of the American society from having full equality? Sometimes it seems that it's only evident to those who are in the fight. Those who are not directly affected or not in the fight appear oblivious to the depth of the struggle – the struggle that has been ongoing since 1640 to today (2020).

Prior to the arrival of slave ships in the early 1600s, most of the colonies had established laws for citizenship. Being British colonies, most used a naturalization policy to establish citizenship. Since the original colonists were the ones making the rules, they made to rules to suit them. As cited in Wikipedia, "Nationality law in the American colonies preceding the *Articles of Confederation* was a decentralized early attempt to develop the concept of citizenship among colonial settlers with respect to the major colonial powers of the period. Precedent was largely based on English common law, with jurisdictional discretion afforded to each of the colonies in accordance with the principles of self-governance. English common law, under principles of *jus sanguinis*, viewed English persons and their children in the colonies as full subjects of the king. English common law was less clear on the status of alien residents in the colonies, who generally faced a difficult naturalization process to obtain the same legal rights inhered to natural-born English and their descendants." This meant that nearly all colonists of British descent could predictably become citizens. However, other nationalities and ethnicities would be allowed citizenship at the discretion of the colonists issuing the documents. The colonist intentionally stayed away from the principles of *jus soli* ("right of soil"), which is solely based on the place of birth. This system gave the colonist discretionary authority on who gained citizenship. Some other specific considerations, in addition to ethnicity, included wealth, skills, religion, and criminal record. It's ironic that these identifiers are still being cited.

Under these proceedings, the Native Americans (American Indians) were not citizens. When African Americans were brought as slaves, they were not viewed as potential citizens. According to Wikipedia, "The emancipation of the slaves forced Americans to define citizenship and the rights that went with it. We took one step closer to creating that 'more perfect Union' by adding three amendments to the Constitution to expand the ideals of liberty and equality upon which the country was built." This statement may be the first untruth about the United States. It is evident as we look at the establishment of the colonies that the intent was established to not form a union with all inhabitants being equal. This is undoubtedly a contentious statement, because it challenges the very foundation of the ideals of the nation.

There were several key events which defined the tone of the nation. In 1640, Negro indentured servant John Punch ran away and received a life sentence in Virginia; his white counterparts (also indentured servants) only received three-year sentences. In 1641, Massachusetts authorized slavery with legislation. In 1662, Virginia determined birthright of Negroes based on the status of the mother rather than the father, as had been the British custom for centuries. (Mixed babies by and large had white fathers and Negro mothers – who often had been raped by the "White master" or his sons). In 1705, Virginia relegated slaves, Indians, and mulattos to the status of property. (Library of Congress...) In 1820, the Missouri Compromise created rules for the expansion of slavery into western territories and prohibited slavery north of the 36° 30´ latitudes, except in Missouri. In 1865, the Thirteenth Amendment to the U.S. Constitution abolished slavery. In 1866, the Civil Rights Act of 1866 guaranteed equal rights under law for all people who lived within the jurisdiction of the United States. In 1868, the Fourteenth Amendment to the U.S. Constitution granted citizenship to all people born or naturalized in the United States and prohibited states from denying any person the equal protection of the laws or depriving any person of life, liberty, or property, without due process of law. In 1870, the Fifteenth Amendment to the U.S. Constitution granted African American men the right to vote. In

1870–1871, Three Enforcement Acts gave the federal government substantial authority to prosecute those who violated the civil and political rights of African Americans, especially members of the Ku Klux Klan.

From the sequence of events outlined above, it would appear that slavery was abolished in 1865, all slaves via birth or naturalization were granted citizenship in 1868, and men were given the right to vote in 1870. Looks great on paper; however, in actuality, this did not go as written. Immediately after the abolishment of slavery, the Ku Klux Klan emerged. From a report by Thought Company, "The Ku Klux Klan was and is undeniably a terrorist organization—but what made the Klan an especially insidious terrorist organization, and a threat to *civil liberties*, was that it functioned as the unofficial paramilitary arm of southern segregationist governments. This allowed its members to kill with impunity and allowed *southern segregationists* to eliminate activists by force without alerting federal authorities. Although the Klan is much less active today, it will be remembered as an instrument of cowardly southern politicians who hid their faces behind hoods, and their ideology behind an unconvincing facade of patriotism. In 1866, the Ku Klux Klan (KKK) was founded. In 1867, Former Confederate general and noted white supremacist Nathan Bedford Forrest, architect of the Fort Pillow Massacre, became the first Grand Wizard of the Ku Klux Klan. The Klan murdered several thousand people in the *former Confederate states* as an effort to suppress the political participation of black Southerners and their allies. In 1868, the Ku Klux Klan published its 'Organization and Principles.' Although early supporters of the Klan claimed that it was philosophically a Christian, patriotic organization, rather than a white supremacist group, a cursory glance at the Klan's catechism reveals otherwise:

1. Are you opposed to Negro equality both social and political?

2. Are you in favor of a white man's government in this country?

3. Are you in favor of constitutional liberty, and a government of equitable laws, instead of a government of violence and oppression?

4. Are you in favor of maintaining the constitutional rights of the South?

5. Are you in favor of the re-enfranchisement and emancipation of the white men of the south, and the restitution of the southern people to all their rights, alike proprietary, civil, and political?

6. Do you believe in the inalienable right of self-preservation of the people against the exercise of arbitrary and unlicensed power?

7. The "inalienable right to self-preservation" is a clear reference to the Klan's violent activities—and its emphasis, even at this early stage, is clearly white supremacy.

In spite of the charter under which the KKK was formed, neither it or other White Supremacy organizations are referred to and violent, war-mongers, or Antifah. However, any activity challenging the government about rights for minority citizen is quickly labeled as violent, anti-patriotic and Antifah affiliated. Martin Luther King Jr. was on the FBI's most wanted list; however, no member of the KKK has ever been wanted by the FBI. Coupled with the formation of the KKK was the enactment of Jim Crow laws by states and municipalities (especially in the south). Examples of Jim Crow laws include:

1. It shall be unlawful to conduct a restaurant or other place for the serving of food in the city, at which white and colored people are served in the same room unless such white and colored persons are effectually separated by a solid partition extending from the floor upward to a distance of seven feet or higher, and unless a separate entrance from the street is provided for each compartment. This law was put in place in 1934.

2. The Alabama constitution of 1901 separated schoolhouses for African Americans and White people.

3. An 1850 California statute provided that no black, mulatto person, or Indian, shall be allowed to give evidence in favor of, or against a white man.

4. All courtships between a white person and a Negro person, or between a white person and a person of Negro descent to the fourth generation inclusive, are hereby forever prohibited.

5. Negroes or mulattoes who intruded into any railroad car reserved for white persons would be found guilty of a misdemeanor. Whites faced the same penalty for entering a car reserved for persons of color.

6. All persons licensed to conduct a restaurant, shall serve either white people exclusively or colored people exclusively and shall not sell to the two races within the same room or serve the two races anywhere under the same license.

7. Building permits for building Negro houses in white communities, or any portion of a community inhabited principally by white people, and vice versa prohibited.

8. Separate but equal accommodations were required to be provided on all forms of public transportation. Separate coaches for white and African American passengers were required on rail.

9. There were to be separate but equal accommodations for whites and African Americans provided in nursing homes.

10. Provided that all persons, firms, or corporations create separate bathroom facilities for members of the white and African American races employed by them or allowed to come into the business. In addition, separate rooms to eat in as well as separate eating and drinking utensils were required to be provided for members of the white and African American races.

11. Every person operating any public hall, theater, opera house, motion picture show or any place of public entertainment or public assemblage, which is attended by both white and colored persons, shall separate the white race and the colored race and shall set apart and designate certain seats therein to be occupied by white persons and a portion thereof, or certain seats therein, to be occupied by colored persons.

12. The Corporation Commission is hereby vested with power and authority to require telephone companies to maintain separate booths for white and colored patrons when there is a demand for such separate booths.

13. That it shall be unlawful for any person, firm, or corporation engaged in the business of cotton textile manufacturing, in this state to

allow or permit operatives, help and labor of different races to labor and work together within the same room, or to use the same doors of entrance and exit at the same time, or to use and occupy the same pay ticket windows or doors for paying off its operatives and laborers at the same time, or to use the same stairway and windows at the same time, or to use at any time the same lavatories, toilets, drinking water buckets, pails, cups, dippers, or glasses.

As if the Jim Crow laws were not bad enough and the formation of the KKK even worst, lynchings ran rampart particularly in the southern states. Data from a study done by the University of Missouri at Kansas City Law School shows the following statistics for recorded lynchings (Blacks/Whites) during the period 1882-1968: Alabama – 299/48, Arkansas – 226/58, Florida – 257/25, Georgia – 492/39, Louisiana – 335/56, Mississippi -529/42, North Carolina – 86/15, South Carolina – 155/4, Tennessee - 204/47 Texas – 352/141(represents non-Blacks includes Hispanic). Some would say this was a long time ago and a different era. Well, I beg to differ; I was nine years old when Emmet Till, a 14-year-old, was lynched in 1955. The end date of the lynching data was 1968. At that time, I was 23 years old and a Captain in the US Army. As a young boy, my parents drilled into me the following: 1) that if I were meeting two White people on the street, make sure that I step aside and give them the entire sidewalk; 2) never walk through a White neighborhood day or night; 3) make sure not to ever look at a White woman; 4) never talk back to a White person, and 5) never ask a white person a question. All of these were things for which Blacks had been lynched.

Many of the Jim Crow laws remained in effect from the 1860s to 1960s. Thus for 100 years after being granted citizenship, that citizenship has never been actualized. Yet today, many of the practices written into Jim Crow laws are still practiced – some written and some unwritten (coded). The KKK has been and remains to be an active organization promoting the same principals listed above. When the term "America" is used, the reference is to White men. Following the passage of the Civil

Rights Act of 1964 and the Voter Rights Act of 1965, the language for maintaining Jim Crow type laws changed to what is now termed "coding" (to be addressed in the next letter). If the Constitution and its amendments were carried out, there would have been no requirement for a Civil Rights Act in 1964 or a Voter Rights Act in 1965. And today efforts are ongoing to rescind/repeal segments of both – along with other legislation is now being reviewed to rescind/repeal.

WHY IS THAT?? NINTH LETTER
A CALL TO SHARE

BLACK CODE

This week, over a 4-day period, I watched the celebration of the Life of Congressman John Lewis. He dedicated his life to the fight for equality. Starting with being arrested at the age of 19, at a Sit-In at Woolworth in Nashville, Tennessee in 1960. During his lifetime, he was severely beaten, handled with high-powered water hoses, and attacked by police attack dogs – multiple times (a total of 40 arrests). He was one of the co-organizers of the March on Washington and a leader in the March across the Edmund Pettus Bridge (the March from Selma to Montgomery).

From 1960 to 2020, many positive actions to advance equality have taken place. Over that 60-year period, the Civil Rights Act of 1964 was passed; the Voter Rights Act of 1965 was passed; and multiple fair housing and equal employment opportunity legislation have been passed. So, we must be exponentially closer to equality in this country than we were 60 years ago.

As I watched the celebration of the life of Congressman, John Lewis, and his dedication to gaining equality for all, I rejoice in his dedication; however, I am saddened when I reflect on all the things that have and are taking place to counter the progress toward equality.

Home ownership is a crucial means by which families can accumulate wealth. Over a period of time, homeowners accumulate *home equity* in their homes. In turn, this equity can contribute substantially to the wealth of homeowners. In summary, home ownership allows for the accumulation of home equity, a means of storing wealth, and provides families with insurance against poverty. Ibarra and Rodriguez state that home equity is 61% of the net worth of Hispanic homeowners, 38.5% of the net worth of White homeowners, and 63% of the net worth of African American homeowners. Conley remarks that differences in rates of home ownership and housing value accrual may lead to lower net worth in the parental generation, which disadvantages the next. There are *large disparities in homeownership rates by race*. In 2017, the home ownership rate was 72.5% for non-Hispanic Whites, 46.1% for Hispanics, and 42.0% for Blacks.

Unfortunately, the efforts to gain equality are frequently countered, rescinded, or neutralized within short order after the forward steps are taken. On 29 July 2020, the President of the United States tweeted the following: "I am happy to inform all of the people living their Suburban Lifestyle Dream that you will no longer be bothered or financially hurt by having low-income housing built in your neighborhood. Your housing prices will go up based on the market, and crime will go down." This message followed the rescission of the AFFH Rule (Affirmatively Furthering Fair Housing Rule). "In July 2015, HUD promulgated the pursuant to the *Fair Housing Act*. It required cities and towns which receive Federal money for any housing or *urban development* related purpose to examine whether there are any barriers to fair housing, housing patterns or practices that promote *bias* based on any protected class under the Fair Housing Act, and to create a plan for rectifying fair housing barriers. The intention is to promote equal housing opportunities and level the playing field so that all neighborhoods provide the quality services and amenities that are important for people to live successful lives. The 2015 rules required cities and towns, in order to receive funding from HUD to document patterns of racial bias in their neighborhoods, to publicly report the results every three to five years, and to set and track goals to reduce segregation." (1968 Fair Housing Act)

In October 1973, the government accused Fred and Donald Trump of violations of the Fair Housing Act of 1968 at 39 Trump-built-and managed buildings in Brooklyn, Queens, and Staten Island. The community groups handed their findings to the Nixon Justice Department on a silver platter. The Trumps were drowning in evidence of systematic racial discrimination. On at least seven occasions, prospective tenants had filed complaints against the Trumps with the human rights commission, alleging racially discriminatory patterns and practices. The ruling was handed down by the United States District Court Eastern District of New York on June 10, 1975. The Trump management company settled with the plaintiffs and agreed to multiple stipulations to never violate the Fair Housing Act of 1968.

Note that this is the same act under which Trump was charged with unfair housing practices in 1973, where his company promised to never violate the Act again. So now that he has rescinded the Act, this legalizes the practice being done prior with unfair housing practices.

Prior to the 1960s, the term "Niggras" (the "N" word) - as pronounced in the south – was used rather freely. As a result of the unrest and activities of the 60s and 70s, that term was verboten. However, instead of removing the term, others have been substituted - "The Black Code". The use of code words serves two or more purposes: 1) intended meaning not recognized by many; 2) the substituted word is not direct, and therefore not legally binding; and 3) a way of communicating the intent without revealing one's true position/feelings/meaning.

There is not a single word that has replaced the N word. Rather, there are multiple words used based on the context in which the conversation is taking place. For example, if the conversation is about young people, the terms may include "Thugs," "Those Young People," "At-Risk," or "Urban Youth" To transmit a strong negative connotation, the term "Thugs" may be used. In a more patronizing conversation, the term "Urban Youth" may be used. In a programmatic or educational conversation, the term "At-Risk" may be used. In all cases, the flow of the conversation is on Black Youth.

Oh, by the way, "Black Codes" did not originate in the 60s. The first recorded era in US history with the use of "Black Codes" dates back to the post-Civil War era. There were several noteworthy take-aways from that era that are manifesting themselves today. Recall that African American men were given the Right to Vote in 1870. However, those rights were basically taken away in 1877 as noted in the Public Broadcasting Service documentary, *Slavery By Another Name*, "Immediately after the Civil War ended, Southern states enacted 'black codes' that allowed African Americans certain rights, such as legalized marriage, ownership of property, and limited access to the courts, but denied them the rights to testify against whites, to serve on juries or in state militias, vote, or start a job without the approval of the previous employer. These codes were all repealed in 1866 when Reconstruction began. But after the failure of Reconstruction in 1877, and the removal of black men from political offices, Southern states again enacted a series of laws intended to circumscribe the lives of African Americans." Although African American men were given the right to vote in 1870, that right was basically taken away with Black Codes and later the Jim Crow laws. This blockage was in affect from 1877 to 1965. Codes used to block the vote: 1) must be a landowner, 2) never arrested, 3) must be able to recite one or more of the following a) Preamble to the Constitution, b) Bill of Rights, and/or c) Declaration of Independence. When my father went to register to vote for the first time in 1957 or '58, he had to recite the Declaration of Independence. My father could not read; therefore, he was not able to register and thus not vote. My father was not an anomaly in the Black community. In many areas he was average to above average – above average because he owned his home. Another mechanism used to keep Blacks from registering to vote was threats that they would lose their jobs, or the bank would foreclose on their loan, or the car dealer would take their car back.

The Voter Rights Act of 1965 removed all the above-mentioned barriers and others. But not so fast, there were more modern barriers initiated: 1) picture IDs, 2) verified address, and 3) no felonies. Many will say these are all very reasonable. Yes, they may be – if they weren't areas where Blacks and other minorities constitute the majority in these categories. Oh, I forgot to mention voting precincts. Well, you see how well the coding works – designed for an intended purpose, yet not revealing its purpose outright.

In 2013, according to *The Guardian:(theguardian.com)*, 25 Jun 2020, "Seven years ago today, the supreme court issued one of the most consequential rulings in a generation in a case called *Shelby county v Holder*. In a 5-4 vote, the court struck down a formula at the heart of the Voting Rights Act, the landmark 1965 law that required *certain states and* localities with a history of discrimination against minority voters to get changes cleared by the federal government before they went into effect."

"It's hard to overstate the significance of this decision. The power of the Voting Rights Act was in the design that the US Supreme Court gutted – discriminatory voting policies could be blocked *before* they harmed voters. The law placed the burden of proof on government officials to prove why the changes they were seeking were not discriminatory. Without the law, voters who are discriminated against now bear the burden of proving they are disenfranchised."

"Immediately after the decision, Republican lawmakers in Texas and North Carolina – two states previously covered by the law – moved to enact new voter ID laws and other restrictions. A federal court would later strike down the North Carolina law, writing it was designed to target African Americans - *with almost surgical precision.*"

In 2020, efforts are still ongoing to repeal segments of the Voter Rights Act of 1965. Thus, this battle to become unencumbered voters continues. You see, if you are not among the disenfranchised, you may not be aware of the constant ongoing battle. For some segments of the US population, the battle for the right to vote ended in 1856 when the Right to Vote was given to "All White Men." Since that time, there have been no efforts to disenfranchise White Men's right to vote. Since 1870 when African American men were given the right to vote, there have been constant efforts to disenfranchise African Americans' right to vote.

This same process of "Black Code" has and is taking place in the areas of housing and employment. The pandemic has revealed something that has constantly been stated for years – that is the inequity in pay and employment.

In the stimulus package that expires July 31, 2020, the Senate and others are debating that the $600 payment exceeds what a significant number of workers would receive if they were working. Therefore, they are reviewing a lesser number to ensure workers have the incentive to return to work. The thing the pandemic reveals is that a significant number of people, although they are working, are making far less than the minimum needed to subsist. Therein lies a major factor — minimum wages do not meet minimum standard of living. And, if at all possible, the effort is and will be to get through the pandemic without addressing raising the minimum wage.

Housing and voting are two of the major areas wherein equality can make a huge difference — positively or negatively. In the case of housing, life for the Zimmermans made a monumental change when my father bought a house in 1954. Two years earlier, he could be denied buying that home. Under the rules just rescinded, he could now again be denied buying that home.

I recently sold a house. Without the Fair Housing Act, I, an African American, could be channeled to receive 20 to 40 thousand dollars less than what my house sold for. You might ask, how is that? Without the AFFH Rule, realtors are unrestricted on selectively guiding potential buyers to certain homes. An African American homeowner is likely to have other African Americans or Hispanics brought to look at their homes than Caucasians or Asians. So as a seller, the potential buyer pool is considerably smaller for an African American than for a Caucasian. Therefore, a Caucasian selling my house could make $20k to $40k more on the same house. What I have just described is not an unusual practice. From the buyer perspective, the realtor is free to channel buyers to certain houses or communities. This places a limitation on market availability and thus denies access. Again, these practices are not published, nor are they followed by everyone. However, it legalizes the discriminatory practice that the Trumps were charged with in 1973. This is why the rescission of the Fair Housing Act of 1968 is so important in the fight for equality.

If your family owned a home at either of these times, these rules would not affect you. However, if your family is in the low-income category and trying to move up, these rulings deny those opportunities for a better life. Therein lies the struggle. Both, the suppression of voter opportunities and housing have a direct impact of the potential for equality in the American society. Those who "have" or are not affected negatively by these actions are fed the fear factor of losing what they have. Throughout my lifetime, that has been the tool to halt or marginalize progress for equality. Prior to the civil war, the fear factor was economic and labor. During the 60s, the fear factors were "those people" are going to take your jobs, marry your daughters, degrade the quality of education....In the 80s and 90s, the fear factors were drugs and education. In the 21st Century, the fear factors are crime, drugs, education, wealth, and "culture change."

What would happen if the fear factors were removed?

The "fear factor" means using fear as a tool to cause people to act in a certain manner. As parents and leaders, we know that parenting by fear or leading by fear are less than optimal and can lead to demise.

TENTH LETTER
A CALL TO SHARE

SYSTEMIC RACISM IN EDUCATION

"In 1954, the Supreme Court ruled in *Brown v. Board of Education* that racial segregation in schools was unconstitutional. The decision is often framed as a landmark decision that transformed education for Black students, allowing them equal access to integrated classrooms. But more than six decades later, *Segregation in American Schools* is still very much a reality", says Rebecca Sibilia, founder of EdBuild, a nonprofit that investigated school funding inequities in America. Her team found, "... predominantly white school districts get collectively $23 billion more per year than predominantly non-white school districts. That's because of another important, but less-studied Supreme Court Case: *Milliken v. Bradley* in 1974. In *Milliken*, the Supreme Court ruled that if a school district line is drawn anywhere for almost any reason, desegregation doesn't have to cross that border. It ultimately has the effect of, in essence, reversing a lot of the impact of *Brown,* entrenched the power of the school district border in desegregation efforts,*"* Sibilia says.

This is another example of what I mentioned in a previous letter – that when a law or bill is passed to eliminate some form of inequality, another bill or law is later passed to negate the previous one. Thus far this has been cited in Voting, Housing, and now Education.

The practice of withholding education from certain minority groups predates the arrival of slaves to America. In fact, it also goes back to the early colonization in Africa. Prior to the colonization of Africa, education of the people was a part of the way of life. As published in *This is*

Africa: What Africa had Before Colonisation, by Philani A. Nyoni in March
2015, "When Europeans arrived in Africa, they found it upon themselves
to bring us commerce and civilization. However, Africa had its own
forms of commerce, science, art and other measures of civilisation long
before the arrival of the colonisers. The healers of Africa were very
knowledgeable about herbs, trees, roots and their medicinal purposes.
One case which well illustrates the greatness of African medicine is that
of childbirth. It is almost certain that we mastered caesarean sections in-
dependently. The Egyptians were so advanced in fields such as astron-
omy, physics and mathematics that the three pyramids of Giza align
directly with the Three Kings constellation, as if it is not amazing enough
that no one alive today has a clear idea on how those monolithic works
of architecture were constructed. A common myth is that Europeans
taught us to read and write. In some parts of Africa that is true, but only
because there was no need for writing. The West Africa region had griots,
wandering human encyclopaedias who were capable of recalling events
and people long – long passed. They were the custodians of history. Py-
thagorus, Aristotle, Piccasso, and others were all beneficiaries of African
innovation. Fractal geometry, the binary system, were used in Africa before the West got a conception of them. In fact, scholars thought they
had reached the epitome of mathematical thought before they were introduced to fractal geometry in Africa."

European colonizers have a history of portraying the occupants of a
new territory that they enter as uncivilized. When in fact, they are just different. In Africa, the climate is very different than Europe. The loin
clothes worn were very adequate; however, difference meant uncivilized
to the Europeans. Because the Africans did not speak or write as they, the
Europeans labeled them as uncivilized. However, with just a little investi-
gatory work, it can be established that the Europeans were being self-
centered (ethnocentric) in their thinking and actions. As a side note, the
riches man ever was an African name Mansa Musa, whose net worth for
exceeded $400 billion. Mansa Musa was King of the Mali Empire during
the period 1280-1337.

As reported in Higher Education Studies, Vol 3, No.4; 2013, in the report, *The African Educational Evolution: From Traditional Training to Formal Education* by Dama Mosweunyane, "Education was seen as a vehicle through which western cultures can be fostered or promoted in the African continent by its colonizers. This arrangement viewed Africans as having little or no knowledge of their own, which meant they had to learn advanced, organised, systematic or sophisticated skills. Therefore, education in Africa cannot be perfectly understood without first understanding the strengths and intentions of the very forces that gnarled it, which according to Mcgregor as cited by Adedeji (1990) was originally motivated by the desire to provide 'moral' upright and honest Christian clerks, traders, interpreters and chiefs. It was also meant to produce Africans who could communicate fluently in the language of the colonial powers."

Next let's briefly review the plight of the Native Americans and their education. "1492: Christopher Columbus lands on a Caribbean Island after three months of traveling. Believing at first that he had reached the East Indies, he describes the natives he meets as 'Indians.' On his first day, he orders six natives to be seized as servants." Between the time of the arrival of Christopher Columbus (1492) and 1850 (358 years), the Native Americans were – not only – not granted citizenship, they were systematically stripped of their land. For a people who were totally dependent on the land for their livelihood and survival, that was devastating. "1851: Congress passes the Indian Appropriation Act, creating the Indian Reservation System. Native Americans weren't allowed to leave their reservations without permission. June 2, 1924: the U.S. Congress passes the Indian Citizenship Act, granting citizenship to all Native Americans born in the territorial limits of the country. Previously, citizenship had been limited, depending on what percentage Native American ancestry a person had, whether they were veterans, or, if they were women, whether they were married to a U.S. citizen."

As I pointed out in the *2019 Partnership with Native Americans* article, "Until 1926, Indian education was viewed as a 'civilizing' or 'assimilation' process. The 'assimilationists' saw the non-reservation boarding school as the best way to make young Indian children accept White men's beliefs and value systems. The most well-known of all the non-reservation boarding schools was the school established in Carlisle, Pennsylvania, by Colonel Richard Henry Pratt in 1879. His goal was complete assimilation:

1) Students had to wear standard uniforms.

    1. Boys had their long hair cut.

    2. Students were given new names.

    3. Traditional foods were abandoned.

    4. Students were not allowed to speak their native languages, even to each other.

Conversion to Christianity was deemed essential. Carlisle had a football team so the boys could learn the American value of winning. Holidays such as Columbus Day, Thanksgiving, New Year's, and Memorial Day were used to further indoctrinate Indian youths into White culture. In the end, parents and students resisted the non-reservations schools and most Indian students did not assimilate into White society."

"Beginning in the 19th Century, there were a number of misguided attempts to educate Native American children. Residential schools, run by religious organizations, were set up, and Native American children were forced to attend. The primary focus of these schools was to assimilate Native American children to dominate the American culture's language, values, and behaviors through a process of deculturalization. Children were forbidden to use their language or engage in Native American customs, in an attempt to replace their culture with the dominant American culture. Unfortunately, residential schools were largely successful in this practice, and some were still in existence up to 1980," as written in the EDVOCATE article, *The Sobering History of Native American Education in the 19th Century* by Matthew Lynch, September 2, 2016.

I realize this was very extensive in covering the education in Early Africa and of Native Americans; however, this sets the pattern of the education process for non-Whites. In all cases, that pattern focused on assimilation into the European/White culture with minimal academic advancement.

During the era of Slavery in America, slaves were denied the opportunity to learn to read or write. In fact, slaves could be hung if they were caught learning to read or write. Of course, slaves could not communicate in their native languages. This combination of no learning and denial of usage of a native language yielded illiteracy. Once the slaves were freed, the view by White America continued that they (the former slaves) were sub-human and thus not capable of learning at the level of Whites. This was established and still is the ethnocentric view toward non-Whites.

Let's fast forward to the period 1950 to 1976. From Wikipedia we find, "Segregation academies are private schools in the Southern United States that were founded in the mid-20th century by white parents to avoid having their children in desegregated public schools. They were founded between 1954, when the U.S. Supreme Court ruled that segregated public schools were unconstitutional, and 1976, when the court ruled similarly about private schools.

While many of these schools still exist – most with low percentages of minority students even today – they may not legally discriminate against students or prospective students based on any considerations of religion, race or ethnicity that serve to exclude non-white students. The laws that permitted their racially discriminatory operation, including government subsidies and tax exemption, were invalidated by U.S. Supreme Court decisions. After *Runyon v. McCrary* (1976), all of these private schools were forced to accept African American students. As a result, 'segregation academies' changed their admission policies, ceased operations, or merged with other private schools.

But most of these schools remain overwhelmingly white institutions, both because of their founding ethos and because tuition fees are a barrier to entry. In communities where many or most white students are sent to these private schools, the percentages of African American students in tuition-free public schools are correspondingly elevated. For example, in Clarksdale, Mississippi, as of 2010, 92% of the students at Lee Academy were white, while 92% of the students are Clarksdale High School were black. The effects of this de facto racial segregation are compounded by the unequal quality of education produced in communities where whites served by former 'segregation academies' seek to minimize tax levies for public schools.

This description of the birth of private schools during the period 1954 to 1976 continues to manifest itself in 2020. There are a few additional descriptors that have been added – two of those are 'home school' and 'church schools.' According to research from UCLA's Civil Rights Project, "...black students are just as segregated today as they were in the 1960s, before serious enforcement of federal desegregation orders went into effect." Many of those in leadership positions at national, state, and local levels (including the U. S. Secretary of Education) are products of the private/home/church schools, yet they are the decision makers and purse-string holders for public education. As it says in Matthew 6:21, "For where your treasure is, there your heart will be also."

Segregated schools and the state of education
is a matter of the heart.
The state of education defines the nation. - Zke

ELEVENTH LETTER:
A CALL TO SHARE

SYSTEMIC RACISM: EDUCATION

Before I begin with the discussion on education, there are a few points I wish to share with the readers. Note that this letter is titled the eleventh and you have not received the tenth. As I was reading over the tenth letter, I had some thoughts I felt compelled to share before sending it. Therefore, you are receiving the eleventh before the tenth.

Some who read these letters may say stop trying to explain racism to people who don't understand it. Their view is that those who don't understand should be investigative enough or observant enough to see the racism. And if they don't get it, it is because they don't want to get it. On the other hand, there are some who read these letters and don't get it. They don't recognize the thrust of the protests; the meaning of the "Black Lives Matter." They will continue to talk in terms of "All Lives Matter," "Blue Lives Matter," etc. This indicates a disconnect in understanding. "Black Lives Matter" is not saying that others' lives do not matter; it's not saying that one person or group's lives matter more than another. It is saying that from as far back as the 14th century, people of color have been systematically treated like their lives do not matter. An analogy that I think about is in dealing with a person who has endured physical and/or mental abuse over an extended period of time. With that person it is counter-productive when they ask do you love me, for the response to be "I love all people." The total effort is for everyone to come to grips with this systemic issue and that Black lives matter just as all others.

The letters – A Call to Share – are just that: God has commissioned to share these words (a testimony). It is not my job to convince anyone; only to provide information. It is up to each person to process it as God so leads them to do. I would be remiss if I did not carry out the commission.

I am led to share the experience which gave me this perspective on life. During the Civil Rights Movement of the 60s, I was arrested many, many times. The last 12 times I was arrested, it was by the Chief of Police. It was my feeling at that time that he hated me so much that he just enjoyed arresting me. All of this was during the four years I was in college. After graduation and being commissioned a second lieutenant in the US Army, I went on active duty with the Army. In August 1966, following my officers' basic course, I reported to Fort Jackson, South Carolina as my initial permanent duty station. At the end of August, I was home (Orangeburg, SC) on a four day leave. That Thursday evening, Alice, my girlfriend at the time, and I went to a movie. When we came out of the move, the Chief of Police was parked in the middle of the street with his blue police light on and beckoned me to his car. I followed our normal procedure: I went over, put both hands on his car, and spread my feet in a position to be search/arrested. He responded that he just wanted to talk. In the conversation, he invited me to have dinner at his house two days later. I was flabbergasted. It was all I could do to maintain my composure and not show how shocked I was. I remained calm and responded, "Let me get back to you on that tomorrow."

I rushed to get Alice home, then go to my house and talk with my dad. I told him about the Police Chief's invitation. His response was, "Well, what are you going to do?" I told him there was no way I was going. I just knew this was a plot to kill me. He then said that I had no choice but to go. He went on to say that if I went and was killed, then the Blacks in my hometown would see where they stood and know what they needed to do; if I weren't killed, this would send a clear message of the progress being made. At that moment, I felt my father's willingness to sacrifice his son. I was one who did whatever my father said – I had complete trust in his judgment. The next day, I called the Chief and accepted the invitation. Then I spent all day Friday, Friday night, and all day Saturday mentally preparing to die Saturday evening when I went to the Chief's house.

My biggest moment was when I parked in front of his house and stepped onto the sidewalk. In my mind, I was convinced that I would be killed on the sidewalk as I approached his house. My rationale was that I had no business at the Chief's house, therefore any jury would find my death as "justifiable homicide." Needless to say, I was not killed nor shot. That was my first time eating in a White person's house. Following dinner as we sat and talked, the Chief said two things to me that changed my outlook: 1) The first thing he said was that he had personally arrested me the last 12 times to ensure my safety. He knew that his officers might not treat me well, so he arrested me to ensure my safety, 2) The second thing he said was that he just hoped that his son would grow up to be the type of man that he saw in me. My life was changed that evening.

The Chief of Police was in his 60s during that time. He was led to go beyond the norm and understand that my life mattered. He went beyond the earthly culture of that time and did what he felt Jesus would do. I am certainly blessed that he was the led by love for his fellowman. Had he only done what was required of him by the city, I don't know what my outcome would have been.

There have been moments that I have wished I could be White not to have to endure the things that I experienced simply because I was Black (being stopped by police for no reason, being followed when in a store, being denied admission to certain facilities, being spoken to in a derogatory manner, etc....) Those moments were short lived. Without the blessings I have had, I am not sure who or what I would be. If I had to live my life over again, I wouldn't change a thing – given the choice to do so. I am extremely blessed to have had the experiences I had.

On the other hand, there are times that I have wished White persons could be Black so they would have the first-hand experiences of the things that many Blacks, Latinos, Native Americans and others have to endure. The irony is that these experiences are not just one-time events;

these experiences are the norm. I have sometimes wished that some White persons could have the experience being Black and having the Police stop them with guns drawn, abusive language and behavior, and having their young children in the car who have to watch as their parents are disrespected and addressed with abusive language.

When I was a child (between the ages of six and 14), we had family prayer every Sunday morning. My father would always pray for those who had plenty. When asked why, his reason was that they have a difficult time understanding what it means to be Christ-like, because they have a hard time sacrificing what material things they have. I figured he was doing that to divert our attention from how poor we were. He always insisted that we walk in the shoes of others to better understand their plight in life. He had us growing up feeling sorry for those who had wealth. There were numerous times my heart would sink when I was with my father and we were in the presence of White persons. He was frequently spoken to in a denigrating manner. Because of the Jim Crow laws and wanting to take care of his family, he took it. I could tell what he was thinking by the look on his face. I sensed that he had flashbacks of being sent to jail by the landowner where we were sharecroppers years earlier. He lived a life of taking that type of treatment. That should not have been, nor should it be. My dad's life matters. I say it because he was always treated like it didn't matter and it should not have been that way.

TWELFTH LETTER
A CALL TO SHARE

SYSTEMIC RACISM IN EDUCATION

As I begin the twelfth letter, I saw a clip on TV a few days ago that rang out on what it takes to have equity in education. The clip was about a parent who developed a pod for learning for their daughter who was entering the first grade. The pod was developed for five families to be included. The family that developed the pod thought beyond their child and thought about the other students. That led them to realize that there are families who don't have the resources to participate in this type learning. The equity piece comes in where the family who developed the pod established that the requirement would be that three of the families in the pod would sponsor two families who did not have the resources. Let's extrapolate that concept – every three families sponsor two families who are less fortunate than they. Imagine, for every three million families who have resources, there would be two million families receiving the support to bring them up to a self-sustaining level.

This requires a HEART of Sacrificial Giving. Ummmm! That's a novel concept – or is it? Leviticus 23:22 "And when you reap the harvest of your land, you shall not reap your field right up to its edge, nor shall you gather the gleanings after your harvest. You shall leave them for the poor and for the sojourner: I am the Lord your God." Hebrews 13:16 "Do not neglect to do good and to share what you have, for such sacrifices are pleasing to God." Acts 2:45 "...and they began selling their property and possessions and were sharing them with all, as anyone might have need." Luke 21:4 "... for they all out of their surplus put into the offering; but she out of her poverty put in all that she had to live on."

The connection between the two paragraphs is having the heart of God. Therein lies the connection with the phrase at the end of the Tenth Letter: *the state of education is a matter of the heart.* I saw sacrifice in 1964 when 14 parents signed their children up to be the first African Americans to attend the all-white schools in Orangeburg, South Carolina. Those parents knew they were subjecting their children to dangerous environments. However, for the good of all, they were willing to sacrifice. Their sacrifices included being spat on, being punched, be cursed at, being slighted in the classroom, and being uncomfortable every day of the school year. Oftentimes, sacrifice includes struggle. It was Fredrick Douglass who said, "If there is no struggle there is no progress. Those who profess to favor freedom and yet deprecate agitation, are men who want crops without thunder and lightning. They want the ocean without the awful roar of its many waters. This struggle may be a moral one, or it may be a physical one, and it may be both moral and physical, but it must be a struggle. Power concedes nothing without demand. It never did and it never will. Men may not get all they pay for in this world, but they must certainly pay for all they get."

As we look at systemic racism in education, some of the specific areas we will address are 1) teachers and teacher preparation, 2) curricula, 3) testing, 4) funding, and 5) specialty programs. In each of these areas, as programs are introduced into the educational system, the programs are presented as progressive measures to improve the current system.

The first area we will address is teachers and teacher preparation. There is a gross disparity in the ratio of teachers and students of the same ethnicity. For example, "racial and ethnic minorities accounted for 20% of all public elementary and secondary school teachers in the United States during the 2015-16 school year", according to data from the National Center for Education Statistics (NCES). That means nearly 80% of teachers are white. Conversely, "by comparison, 51% of all public elementary and secondary school *students* in the U.S. were nonwhite in 2015-16", the most recent year for which NCES has published data. This data gets even more interesting when looking at urban public schools. As pointed out earlier in the discussion of private schools, many urban public schools now have 80%+ of minority students. "Larger shares of teachers were nonwhite at schools with more nonwhite students, while the reverse was true for schools with more white students. For instance, nonwhites made up 55% of teachers in schools where at least 90% of students were nonwhite. By comparison, across schools where at least 90% of students were white, nearly all teachers (98%) also were white," as cited by NCES. There are numerous implications from these statistics. The first observation is that in no setting does the ratio of non-white teachers match that of non-white students. The second observation is that white students, regardless of the setting, always have a greater or at least equal ratio of white teachers.

In 2002, I was the assistant principal in a high school in Virginia. There the ethnic ratio of teachers was 78 white teachers (75%) and 26 non-white (25%); the ethnic ratio of students was 42% white and 58% non-white. After moving to another city while serving as the Assistant Principal in an "urban" high school with 62% of the student body being African American, the teachers' population was 47 white and 15 non-white. In 2011, while serving as the Assistant Principal in a different "urban" high school in the same city with 67% of the student body being African American, the teachers' population was 46 white and 12 non-white.

The significance of the ratio of teachers by ethnicity is the impact that same ethnicity and role modeling has on student outcomes. This becomes even more when we explore ethnicity and gender. In the case of the first high school, the non-white female teachers constituted 16% of the faculty and white female teachers were 56%; the non-white female students were 40% of the student body. This example is not unusual for high schools. The disproportion gets even greater at the elementary level.

As reported by Jessica Fregni in the June 13, 2019, article *Students Benefit from Having Teachers Who Look Like Them* in Teach For America, "Studies show that students do, indeed, benefit from teachers who look like them. Black students who have even one black teacher by third grade are 13 percent more likely to enroll in college, according to research from Johns Hopkins University and American University. These same researchers also found that the positive 'role model effect' of having a teacher who looks like you was especially beneficial for low-income young Black men, who are 39 percent less likely to drop out of high school if they had at least one black teacher in elementary school. Other research has found that students also benefit from attending schools led by principals of color. At the same time, however, although nearly eight in 10 public school students identifies as a person of color, only about one in five teachers do so, according to recent national data on the demographic breakdown of teachers and students." Ted Gregory in his Chicago Tribune Article, 25 July 2018, reported, "…Black students with Black teachers were suspended less often than Black students with white or Hispanic teachers." He also reported on "the role model effect," "… a Black male student merely having one Black teacher in elementary school led to an increased expression of interest in college and increased the number of Black students taking a college entrance exam by 10 percent." The fact of fewer suspensions means students are in class more, which in turn facilitates learning, which facilitates achievement.

So, it should be evident that a major issue with the population of teachers is lack of balance on the ratio (by ethnicity and gender) of teachers to the respective category of students. There is little evidence any major efforts are going to rectify this systemic shortcoming. One example of an ongoing program to change this dynamic is the "Call Me Mister" Program. As defined by Clemson University, home of the program, "The mission of the Call Me MISTER® (acronym for Mentors Instructing Students Toward Effective Role Models) Initiative is to increase the pool of available teachers from a broader more diverse background particularly among the State's lowest performing elementary schools. Student participants are largely selected from among underserved, socioeconomically disadvantaged, and educationally at-risk communities. The project provides:

• Tuition assistance through Loan Forgiveness programs for admitted students pursuing approved programs of study in teacher education at participating colleges.
 • An academic support system to help assure their success.
 • A cohort system for social and cultural support.
 •Assistance with job placement.

On a national level, the "Call Me Mister" Program is in Georgia at Georgia College, Illinois at University of Illinois at Chicago, Kansas at Kansas State University, Kentucky at Eastern Kentucky University, Louisiana at Louisiana Tech University and Northwestern University of Louisiana, Tennessee at University of Tennessee Martin, Texas at University of Houston Downtown, and Virginia at Longwood University. Although this program is in several states, it is ultra-significant to note that NONE of the host universities is an HBCU (another indicator of system racism). Here is a program aimed at increasing the number of teachers from diverse backgrounds (similar to the students), yet the program is housed in predominantly white universities (PWU). This is an obvious issue because the targeted population to participate in this program are more likely to attend an HBCU than a PWU.

The hint is there needs to be a national effort to correct the disparity in the ethnic and gender ratios of teachers – especially in the elementary school. The programs must be established based on research and needs – not on who writes the best grant. Again, this is a national issue which requires a national solution.

The next four to six letters will each address one of the major factors contributing to systemic racism in the area of education.

THIRTEENTH LETTER
A CALL TO SHARE

SYSTEMIC RACISM IN EDUCATION:
TESTING

"If your response to an unarmed black man getting shot seven times in the back in front of his children is to ask what he did to deserve that, you really need to stop insisting that all lives matter to you," Facebook, 25 August 2020, Unarmed Black Man Shot by Kenosha Wisconsin Police Seven Times in the Back with his Kids in the Car. Although this is not the subject of this lesson, I felt compelled to share and comment. Our country is at a pivotal point. We need to acknowledge that killing other human beings is not OK, especially when no one else's life is being threatened or when other actions can be taken to halt a threatening act or activity. It isn't OK for our police to have to be subjected to unsafe environments. It is not OK for looting, rioting, or destruction of property. It is not OK for police to shoot anyone who is not imposing life threatening situations on others. With regard to what's happening currently, a key factor is identifying the cause. The Lieutenant Governor of Wisconsin was on target when he pointed out how the prevailing rhetoric is encouraging vigilante type behaviors. It's important that the perpetrators committing the acts of violence be properly identified in the protest demonstrations. Incorrect identifications often-time lead to much more widespread negative actions which could be avoided. Again, we have the generalizations being made – these protesters are thugs, unlawful, un-American...and the list goes on. This rhetoric plants the seed that ALL PROTESTERS fall into this category. This situation was further exacerbated by the praising and celebrating a couple who stood in front of their home with guns pointed at protesters who were passing their home in a gated community. The couple's actions gained them a spot for speaking at the Republican National Convention. It is imperative that we connect the dots and realize that praising such behavior validates the actions of the 17-year-old who shot two protesters.

Now for the topic of this letter: Systemic Racism in Education in the area of testing. This topic includes multiple facets of testing: 1) subject matter testing for classes, and 2) college entrance testing – SAT and ACT. NEITHER of the above testing categories serve in favor of minority students or minority teachers, rather standardized testing in the classroom and the SAT are hindrances.

At one point, students' grades depended on their assignments, participation and tests – all generated by the classroom teacher. Granted, this does not lend itself to comparing the learning of students in different classes, different schools, different cities, different states, nor different countries. This did serve to the students' advantage because the teacher is best positioned to know the students and how to measure the students' learning. Over time the grading based on the teacher's assignments and teacher designed tests has diminished significantly. The system has moved much more in the direction of standard testing for students. The tragedy is this DOES NOT measure nor facilitate student learning. Instead, it has promoted test taking skills and teaching for tests. Teachers are figuring out what they need to teach in order for students to do well on tests.

Resources for Teachers reported in an article, *Examining the Pros and Cons of Standardized Testing*, June 29, 2019, by Derrick Meador, the following: "Regardless of the diversity of opinion, there are some common arguments for and against standardized testing in the classroom. Proponents of standardized testing say that it is the best means of comparing data from a diverse population, allowing educators to digest large amounts of information. They argue that: 1) it's accountable (educators and schools are responsible for teaching students what they are required to know for these standardized tests); 2) it's analytical (without standardized testing, this comparison would not be possible); 3) it's structured (standardized testing is accompanied by a set of established standards or an instructional framework to guide classroom learning and test preparation); 4) it's objective (tests are developed by experts, and each question undergoes an intense process to ensure its validity – that it properly assesses the content – and its reliability, which means that the question tests consistently over time); and, 5) it's granular (the data generated by testing can be organized according to established criteria or factors, such as ethnicity, socioeconomic status, and special needs)." Note that all the "pros" for standardized testing focus on facilitating comparing students or groups and the ability to generate data. The thing that is absent in the pros is how it enhances student learning. The reason for the absence is that it doesn't enhance or increase student learning.

Next, let's review the cons of standardized testing. From the same article as cited in the previous paragraph, "Opponents of standardized testing say educators have become too fixated on scores and preparing for these exams. Some of the most common arguments against testing are: 1) it's inflexible (some students may excel in the classroom yet not perform well on a standardized test because they're unfamiliar with the format or develop test anxiety; family strife, mental and physical health issues, and language barriers can all affect student's test score; 2) it's a waste of time (standardized testing causes many teachers to teach to the tests, meaning they only spend instructional time on material that will appear on the test; 3) it can't measure true progress (standardized testing only evaluates one-time performance instead of a student's progress and proficiency over time; 4) it's stressful (teachers and students alike feel test stress; for educators, poor student performance may result in a loss of funding and teachers being fired; for students, a bad test score may mean missing out on admission to the college of their choice or even being held back; 5) it's political (with public and charter schools both competing for the same public funds, politicians and educators have come to rely even more on standardized test scores; some opponents of testing argue that low-performing schools are unfairly targeted by politicians who use academic performance as an excuse to further their own agendas)." Now note that the cons for standardized testing focus on the students and teachers. So, the question to be answered becomes very simple – Should the education system be designed for students' learning and teachers' teaching, or should it be designed for data analyst and politicians?

The disparity in the use of standardized testing would be less noticeable if schools had a relatively equal distribution based on ethnicity and socioeconomics. When you have a school with 90% low socioeconomic and minority students, that school is unlikely to have comparable test scores with a school of mid to high socioeconomics and majority white. This feeds right into that dialogue that argues Black students cannot learn as well as White students. Even before testing, we saw how segregated schools are and how these schools received fewer resources. Standardized testing helps to justify under-resourcing.

The standardized testing helps to spotlight those low-performing schools (as defined by the test). Publicizing these "low-performing" schools increases the argument from parents to keep their children from attending such schools. Many teachers don't wish to teach in these schools.

Therefore, standardized testing serves as a catalyst to the downward spiral of low-performing schools. Some will argue that these schools need to be eliminated. What about the students? One would hope that the system would be about helping promote the education of these students. Rather, the system is aiding (systemic racism) in the lessening of educating certain students. To eliminate or at least reverse the systemic racism, the need is to revamp the standardized testing system which is being expanded rather than diminished.

Next, let's turn our attention to the SAT and ACT and how they impact the education of minorities. Gloria Bonilla-Santiago, HuffPost Contributor, Founder, LEAP Academy University Charter School, Camden, New Jersey; *The SAT: Not an Effective Measuring Stick for Urban Students* wrote, "Consider this: Blacks and Hispanics are well behind the 43 percent of students overall who met the 1,550-point college-readiness barometer last year — a percentage has remained virtually unchanged for five years, according to the College Board, which administers the SAT. The SAT or ACT is increasingly proving to be out of touch anachronistic test that does not provide a full picture of a minority student's potential."

The USA Today High School Sports, *The Effectiveness of the SAT*, by Taylor D'Aprile, October 26, 2015, stated, "Failure to excel in standardized tests limits these students' options for universities, ultimately affecting many aspects of their later life. The importance of these tests should be reevaluated considering their numerable downfalls and complications, so that students who do not fit into the regulations of standardized society can find success and reassurance."

"The SAT, more than anything else, shows how well you take the SAT," said Edward Carroll, a standardized test expert and tutor at the *Princeton Review* who has taken the SAT for the past decade. In an interview with *The Washington Post*, Carroll noted that the SAT is "NOT a measure of student's raw math or verbal ability. The College Board [which owns the test] itself does not claim that the SAT predicts subject skills, but rather that it is a predictor of performance in college (along with the rest of a student's application). Personally, I think it also filters out students who can't perform quickly. The test is rigidly and tightly timed." Carroll also called the SAT a "very flawed test" in terms of revealing student content skill or personal study and performance ability. "The SAT puts students in a pressurized environment," he explained, "and students who perform well in testing situations will excel on the SAT, if you're brilliant and slow, you'll get a very average score."

Although it is widely recognized that the SAT is biased toward students who are good test takers and those who have the resources to get extra help preparing for the test, there is no evidence of any movement to remove the biases and level the playing field to provide equal opportunity for students who do not fit the standardized test model.

The bottom line for this letter is that both, the standardized classroom testing and the college entrance testing – SAT and ACT, contribute to the systemic racism endured by minority students. This is another piece of the systemic racism puzzle that prevents the equal opportunity that we claim/seek. This is not to say that this hinders all minorities. However, it is saying that it hinders the majority of minority students. It's systemic because it is woven into the entire system and accepted as the norm for the entire society. Thus, a minority child is impacted by this bias the moment he/she enters the educational system, beginning in kindergarten.

FOURTEENTH LETTER
A CALL TO SHARE

SYSTEMIC RACISM IN EDUCATION:
CURRICULUM

"We are a nation of fierce, proud, and independent American patriots. We are a nation of pilgrims, pioneers, adventurers, explorers, and trailblazers who refuse to be tied down, held back, or in any way reigned in. Americans have steel in their spines, grit in their souls, and fire in their hearts. There is no one like us on Earth. I want every child in America to know that you are part of the most exciting and incredible adventure in human history. No matter where your family comes from, no matter your background in America, anyone can rise with hard work, devotion, and drive. You can reach any goal and achieve every ambition.

"Our American ancestors sailed across the perilous ocean to build a new life on a new continent. They braved the freezing winters, crossed the raging rivers, scaled the rocky peaks, trekked the dangerous forests, and worked from dawn till dusk. These pioneers didn't have money. They didn't have fame. But they had each other. They loved their families, they loved their country, and they loved their God. When opportunity beckoned, they picked up their Bibles, packed up their belongings, climbed into their covered wagons, and set out West for the next adventure.

"Ranchers and miners, cowboys and sheriffs, farmers and settlers. They pressed on past the Mississippi to stake a claim in the wild frontier. Legends were born: Wyatt Earp, Annie Oakley, Davy Crockett, and Buffalo Bill. Americans built their beautiful homesteads on the open range. Soon, they had churches and communities, then towns, and with time, great centers of industry and commerce." Donald J. Trump, Republican National Convention, Republican Presidential Nomination Acceptance Speech, 27 August 2020.

I included this quote to highlight how Blacks and Native Americans are omitted from being included when we view the history of the United States. Neither of these two groups was acknowledged by the President as being a part of the building of the United States. The groups included are "Anglo." If a listener is in the "Anglo" group, they are likely to feel included; if a listener is in the Black or Native American group, there is likely the feeling of being not included – not part of the building of the US, not essential, etc....This is not different from the school curriculum that all students have for US history from kindergarten through college. The details of Native Americans in the history of the US are not included. Details of slavery in America are also missing from the history books.

"The ancestors of living Native Americans arrived in what is now the United States at least 15,000 years ago, possibly much earlier," *Wikipedia, Native Americans in the United States.* "There are 574 federally recognized tribes living within the US, about half of which are associated with Indian reservations. After its formation, the United States, as part of its policy of settler colonialism, continued to wage war and perpetrated massacres against many Native American peoples, removed them from their ancestral lands, and subjected them to one-sided treaties and to discriminatory government policies, later focused on forced assimilation, into the 20th century. Since the 1960s, Native American self-determination movements have resulted in changes to the lives of Native Americans, though there are still many contemporary issues faced by Native Americans. Today, there are over five million Native Americans in the United States."

Scholastic 100 cites the following (not all inclusive) contributions Native Americans made to the development of the United States: "1) Government: Native American governments in eastern North America, particularly the League of the Iroquois, served as models of federated representative democracy to the Europeans and the American colonists. The United States government is based on such a system, whereby power is distributed between a central authority (the federal government) and smaller political units (the states). 2) Mathematics: The Mayans of Mexico appear to have been the first to use the zero in mathematics. 3) Medicine: The Quechua peoples of Peru discovered the medicinal use for quinine. Also, Canadian Indians knew how to prevent scurvy by eating plants rich in vitamin C, and they passed this information along to the Europeans. 4) Animals: Native Americans were the first to raise turkeys, llamas, guinea pigs, and honeybees for food. 5) Food: Edible plants domesticated by Native Americans have become major staples in the diets of peoples all around the world. Such foods include corn (maize), manioc, potatoes, sweet potatoes, peanuts, squashes and pumpkins, tomatoes, papayas, avocados, pineapples, guavas, chili peppers, chocolate (cacao), and many species of beans. 6) Non-Edibles Plants: Other plants of great importance developed by Native Americans include cotton, rubber, and tobacco." The history books speak extensively about the value of cotton, rubber, and tobacco in building the US economy. A few other inventions by Native Americans as cited in the History Newsletter, *Ten Native American Inventions Used Today* 18 November 2019, "Kayaks, snow goggles, cable suspension bridges, raised-bed agriculture, baby bottles, hammocks, oral contraceptives, syringes, and mouth wash." "People don't realize the ingenuity or the knowledge that native people had, and continue to have about the world around them," explains Gaetana De Gennaro, a supervisory specialist at the National Museum of the American Indian in New York, who manages a permanent interactive exhibit on Native American inventions.

Keisha L. Bentley-Edwards, an assistant professor of educational psychology in the College of Education at The University of Texas at Austin, pointed out in her article, *We Need to Change How We Teach Black History*, in Time Magazine 2020, "School children, as well as adults, should understand the breadth of black heritage. When we study any other group, we recognize the fullness of their humanity. Just as we should never forget the pain of the Holocaust when we talk about Jewish history, we do not often begin discussions with that horrific event. When you recognize a group's humanity, you understand that these historical moments were preceded by their own socio-historical contexts." She continues, "Enslaved Africans brought culture and norms with them that impacted their language, diet and spirituality. When enslaved Africans are described as slaves instead of as humans, the harms they suffered are diminished."

If one does not know the contributions that African Americans have made to the development of America, that can easily be found by looking it up (Google). So, I won't dwell on the contributions. What I will key on is the importance of the inclusion of the heritage and experiences of both the Native Americans and African Americans in the history books.

The absence of the details about Native Americans and African Americans leaves white students without the knowledge base to understand these two groups. This lack of understanding leads to inadequate interpersonal skills to maximize the depth of relationships with them. A sterling example of this is the military in the '70s when an inordinate amount of resources was used to implement Equal Opportunity training and awareness. This resulted from white officers, at all levels, not being prepared to deal with the issues facing African American personnel in their commands. The same was the experience in the business and corporate worlds. The same exists today. Practically every corporation or large business has an Equal Opportunity person at the executive level. Again, this is because the top-level executives do not possess the understanding of the minorities to maximize their utilization and inclusion in the organization. This lack of understanding began in elementary school and was not addressed at any level in the educational process. The top is too deep to attempt to introduce and master it in a three to six week training program.

In addition to being unprepared to lead minorities under their leadership umbrella or under their command, white leaders tend then to marginalize their minority subordinates – oftentimes not realizing that this is taking place. It is, in fact, taking place out of ignorance resulting from not being educated in the history of the minorities. The history and American culture, more often than not, portrays Native Americans and African Americans as renegades, thugs, uneducated, simpletons....Those who don't learn, or are not exposed to, the history of minorities have no basis then for negating the images they see on TV, in the movies, and from their parents. It's ironic that the minorities then generally have a broader exposure base to the history than the whites. This contributes significantly to the ethnocentric view that often is exhibited by White/Anglo Americans. That is the case in nearly every place that whites have gone and the land was occupied by another culture upon their arrival.

Janeane Davis, President and Chief Executive Officer of James, Davis and Associates, in the February 2, 2016, issue of SheKnows Media summarized the need to incorporate African American and Native American history in the school curriculum. "When students are taught black history in school, they get an understanding of many different types of people. In many cases, they will see similarities between African Americans and people of other races. Additionally, they will learn that there are some cultural differences between African Americans and people of other races.

"This is a good thing. The similarities will show that African Americans are not to be feared, shunned or avoided. It is good to learn about cultural differences because it will show that, just as siblings have differences but are still part of the same family, African Americans are part of the United States. When students are taught that African Americans who live in their country are somehow strange, should be feared and not as valuable as other races, it is easy for those students to be afraid of people of other races living in countries around the world. This attitude can lead to misunderstanding, xenophobia and even war. Learning about black history fosters cultural appreciation and fights against xenophobia."

Bottom line: to minimize or eliminate the contribution the current school curriculum is making to perpetuating systemic racism requires a wholesale revamping of the history being taught in schools. That revamping does not require eliminating the current material; it does require infusing the history of Native Americans and African Americans into the current history. Students (white and black) need to learn about life as a slave during the pre- and post- civil war era. Students need to learn about the migration of blacks from the south to the north – just as we learned about the Europeans coming to America and the movement to the west. Students need to learn about the life of Native Americans before the arrival of the colonist, and then their history after the arrival of the colonist – especially the history of the Native Americans as it relates to the colonists' movement to explore the western frontier. It is difficult for one to engage in a comprehensive study of history and not change their appreciation for the contributions that Native Americans and African Americans made to the development of the United States.

FIFTEENTH LETTER
A CALL TO SHARE

SYSTEMIC RACISM IN EDUCATION:
A NEED TO STUDY BLACK HISTORY

I am including the picture below to emphasize the importance of education – not only for minorities, but for all.

This picture appeared on Facebook, 7 September 2020

I felt a need to address the content in this picture as we discuss the importance of education. The first point in the picture is that: "…an ethnic group has Black Awareness Month…" Hopefully, those who question "Black History Month" would ask the question – why have a Black History Month? There are several aspects to the answer: 1) American History classes do not recognize the vast contributions of Blacks to American History, 2) American History books do not approach adequately covering the suffering of Blacks in America while significantly contributing to the growth of the United States, 3) Blacks need to be more aware of their history, and 4) Whites need to learn Black History and recognize the contributions.

"One purpose of Black History Month is to recognize black people who have achieved unthinkable things as well as recognize their progress in achievements and culture. It is important to remind people all over the world, not just in America, that white men are not the only people contributing to the future." Odyssey, *Why Black History Month Is Important*, by Rachael Sanders, Purdue University, February 16, 2016.

"Black history month is a necessary month. There are very few black history classes in public schools. All that is covered is a chapter then black history is forgotten about altogether.

"It is imperative that we remember our past. Those that don't know their history are doomed to repeat it. It is often perceived that African Americans have done nothing for our society, so each generation of black youth needs to understand the struggle and sacrifices our predecessors endured to achieve equal rights and tolerance in American society. "The George-Anne Media Group, *Why Black History Month is Important,* by Charles Rudison, February 4, 2014.

"A cultural month for a minority group is different. It's about acknowledging triumph over adversity. Namely, the adversity that has benefited white Americans and white people for centuries." Splinter, Why Black History Month Is Important, by Amy Stretten, February 20, 2014.

The second point from the picture is – "Black Only Colleges." This is a very interesting statement. First and foremost, the reason "Black Colleges" were established is because Blacks were not allowed to attend "White Colleges." "HBCUs established prior to the American Civil War include Cheyney University of Pennsylvania in 1837 and Lincoln University in 1854. Wilberforce University was also established prior to the American Civil War; it was founded in 1856 via a collaboration between the African Methodist Episcopal Church of Ohio and the Methodist Episcopal Church (the latter a predominantly white denomination). Wilberforce was the third college to be established in the state of Ohio." "In 1862, the federal government's Morrill Act provided for land grant colleges in each state. Some educational institutions established under the Morrill Act in the North and West were open to blacks. But 17 states, mostly in the South, required their systems to be segregated and generally excluded black students from their land grant colleges." *Historically black colleges and universities,* from Wikipedia, the free encyclopedia. The private Black colleges which opened prior to and subsequent to the Civil War never denied admittance to Whites or other ethnic groups. The land grant institutions in the south were required by the states' legislatures to be segregated (Black only). As a South Carolina native, I graduated from high school in May 1962. At that time, no white college in South Carolina would admit a person of color. As reported in the State Newspaper, January 28, 1963, "Harvey Gantt leaves the Registrar's Office at Clemson College (now Clemson University) in January 1963. Gantt was the first African American student to be admitted to Clemson as well as the first to be enrolled at a previously all-white public institution in the state of South Carolina. "Meanwhile, the legislature of the state of South Carolina withdrew its requirement that South Carolina State College remain segregated just two years earlier. It is interesting to note that Strom Thurmond, a staunch segregationist, enrolled his daughter at South Carolina State College in the 1940's. As recorded in Wikipedia, "Essie Mae Washington-Williams (October 12, 1925 – February 4, 2013) was an American teacher, author, and writer. She is best known as the eldest child of Strom Thurmond, Governor of South Carolina (1947–1951) and longtime United States Senator, known for his pro–racial segregation policies. She started college at the all-black South Carolina State College (SCSC) in the fall of 1947. Thurmond quietly paid for her college education."

The third phrase on the flyer at the beginning is "…their Black only dating sites, bars and clubs." Again, it should be noted that prior to the 1970s, Blacks were not allowed in "white bars and clubs" – especially country clubs. On September 11, 1990, the Los Angeles Times reported, "The Augusta National Golf Club, site of the Masters tournament, has accepted its first black member." The Dallas news, CBSN Dallas-Ft Worth, reported, "Founded in 1896, The Dallas Country Club in Highland Park has never had an African American member, until now, February 14, 2014." In 2020, there are still some clubs that will not accept people of color as members.

The bottom line is the above flyer ignores the facts of Blacks being denied entry or membership in "All White" establishments even though the constitution and multiple court actions directed otherwise. In very remote cases does any "black only" establishment exist. The cases cited of black-only universities, the state legislators (white controlled) mandated that they be segregated. The private black universities had no such restrictions going back to the first black college. "The first and oldest HBCU, Cheyney University, was founded in 1837 in Pennsylvania. At the time, Blacks were not allowed to attend most colleges and postsecondary institutions, as a result of slavery and segregation." BBC News, by Cache McClay, *The Story of Historically Black Colleges in the US*, 15 February 2019.

All of the areas shown on the opening flyer are indicators of a need for education. Education would have enlightened the flyer's creator and followers that several of these categories are the direct result of racist acts, which prevente¹ blacks from participating with Whites – college/university and clubs. These are again cases where the constitution – "We the people" (but not blacks or Native Americans) – provided access. The US History books portray America, to include the "wild west," being developed by whites with negligible contributions by blacks and Native Americans.

The opening flyer indicates a lack of knowledge or ignoring the obvious. In either case, this perpetuates the long existing (>400 years) of racism endured in these United States. An effort to ignore the history by turning the table is somewhat pervasive throughout time. That's like saying, "slavery went away over 150 years ago, just get over it." Well, first, it has never totally gone away.

"Equality is the reflection of a just, sensible society." – Unknown
"Until we get equality in education, we won't have an equal society."
– Sonia Sotomayor

"Equality and separation cannot exist in the same space."
– Jason Mraz

"We will never have true civilization until we have learned to recognize the rights of others."
–Will Rogers

"A child miseducated is a child lost." – John Kennedy
"Whatever is my right as a man is also the right of another."
– Thomas Paine

"Giving someone else equal rights does not infringe or take away rights from you. It just makes it illegal to enforce your prejudice and hate."
— Unknown

SIXTEENTH LETTER
A CALL TO SHARE

SYSTEMIC RACISM IN EDUCATION:
FUNDING AND SPECIALITY PROGRAMS

In many school systems, the areas of funding and specialty programs are inseparably intertwined. Specialty programs come in the form of programs within a school, career and technical programs and schools, separate public schools, and public charter schools. Some examples of specialty programs include: Immersion programs (e.g., French, Spanish, and Chinese), International Baccalaureate (IB) Program, Talented & Gifted (TAG), Science, Technology, Engineering and Math (STEM), and Aviation. Some examples of specialty schools include: Montessori, Creative & Performing Arts, and Career and Technical.

As pointed out in article, *The Ongoing Debate Over School Choice*, in the Public School Review, February 10, 2020 by Grace Chen, "There are many arguments made in favor of school vouchers today. Some of these assertions include:

• School vouchers empower parents to make choices for their children, based on their children's unique needs, interests and learning styles.

• School vouchers eliminate the need for parents to pay twice for their children's education: once in tax dollars and again in tuition costs.

• School vouchers meet children's needs more effectively by allowing them to go to the school that is the best fit for them, rather than the one that is simply in the neighborhood.

• The government-run education system currently isn't working;

schools are failing, and students are falling through the cracks.

• A voucher system promotes competition between area schools, which raises the bar on the standard of education throughout all schools, including public schools.

• Vouchers offer students in low-income areas with poorly performing schools a chance at a better education and the opportunity to break the cycle of poverty."

She continues, "While the potential benefits of school vouchers are great, there are many drawbacks to the system as well. Those who oppose a school voucher system often present the following arguments against vouchers:

• School vouchers take money away from the public school system — and budgets currently are so tight in many school districts across the country, additional cuts could seriously undermine the value of public education today.

• Because many private schools are religious, the allowance of using tax dollars to pay for private schools that subscribe to a particular faith is a blatant violation of the constitutional separation of church and state.

• Vouchers do not benefit all students, since private schools still have the ability to pick and choose which students attend and could discriminate against certain students if they so choose.

• With more schools vying for tuition money, the quality of private schooling may suffer in the process, leaving some parents actually paying out of pocket for a lesser education than they would get from public schools.

• School vouchers skim the best students away from the public school system, making it that much more difficult for public schools to make the grade on standardized test scores and get subsequent funding for higher scores.

• A school voucher system tends to divide the country, while public education serves to unite it."

Many of the pros and cons for vouchers equally apply to the discussion of the pros and cons for specialty programs, specialty schools, and charter schools. Just as vouchers take away funds from the public schools, specialty programs and specialty schools also take money away from the comprehensive school. First let's explore the impact specialty programs have on the public school. The cost per student in the specialty program is greater than the cost per student in the regular school setting. However, the appropriations to the school are not computed based on the specialty program. Thus, the presence of the specialty program requires taking some funds from the non-specialty students to fund the specialty program(s). The more specialty programs there are in a school system, the more funds have to be taken from the non-specialty students.

Funding is one aspect. Another aspect of specialty programs is the student selection process for the programs. Several methods we will explore are 1) academic achievement, 2) lottery, 3) audition/portfolio, and 4) open enrollment.

Some of the specialty programs/schools have academic criteria for selection/admittance, such as International Baccalaureate (IB) and Science, Technology, Engineering and Math (STEM). In the article, *Why We Say "Opportunity Gap" Instead of "Achievement Gap,"* in Teach For America, Top Issues, May 11, 2018, by Theresa Mooney, "We've stopped saying 'achievement gap' when referring to the difference in academic performance between students from low-income communities and those from affluent areas—and here's why you should, too. 'Opportunity gap' refers to the fact that the arbitrary circumstances in which people are born—such as their race, ethnicity, ZIP code, and socioeconomic status—determine their opportunities in life, rather than all people having the chance to achieve to the best of their potential. Simply stated, we believe the term 'achievement gap' unfairly places blame on kids. Rather it's A Systemic Problem—Not a Kid Problem. We think the causes of these differences are unequal and inadequate educational opportunities, not inherent differences in capability or character." The achievement/opportunity gap is the major factor in the specialty programs where academic criteria is the requisite for selection/acceptance. What this means then is that the student with greater resources (race, economics, zip code, and ethnicity) has the advantage in the selection process when compared to the student with the lesser resources – when both possess the same potential. I had the opportunity to see this play out in one of my schools when I sat in on the IB selection committee as they developed the criteria for accepting students. I compared my credentials when I was in high school to their criteria, and it was quickly obvious that I would have been an unlikely candidate for this program (a reject). Yet, as I sat there, I reflected that I graduated number two in my college class with a major in mathematics, graduated with a master's degree in Industrial Engineering from Georgia Tech, and received a doctoral degree from George Washington University. So, I could just see the type of students who would be denied selection yet have the potential to be very successful. For this and many other programs that have requirements for selection, "open access" is required for students like me to be able to get into them.

Next, the lottery approach for student selection. "Openings are limited in all Specialty Programs. Availability differs by program, location, and grade level. **Submission of an application is not a guarantee of placement**. All applications are given a waiting list number based on their Specialty Program choice, grade level, and sequence number. The computerized lottery system will assign a random number to each application. Applications are sorted based on this randomly assigned number and assign a sequential number. The lowest random number is assigned number one, the next lowest number two, and so forth. Applications are then sorted by program. Placements are then made on space availability basis only." Prince George's County Public Schools, Prince George's County, Maryland, 2019. This process for lottery selection is the common example from many school districts. So, what's the negative of this form of selection? Again, the "Opportunity Gap" comes into play. The student from the environment with fewer resources and opportunities is less likely to have the parent/guardian involvement necessary to maximize her/his chances for applying and meeting deadlines.

Last let's explore the impact of gifted programs and the requirement for audition and portfolios:

In the New York City, 2020-2021 School Year, *2020 Specialized High Schools Student Handbook*, **we find,** "Use the information, tips, and practice tests in this book to prepare for the summer 2020 SHSAT and La-Guardia High School auditions."

The Education Corner, *Pros and Cons of Gifted Learning Programs in Schools, by Becton Loveless,* Copyright 2020 Educationcorner.com., gives several points on the downside of specialty programs:

• "The majority of parents want their children to participate in a school gifted education program. It makes parents feel good to know that their child is considered 'gifted' and most people believe that being gifted places kids on a path toward success. The truth, however, is more complicated. Although there are distinct benefits of gifted education, there are also some potentially serious problems.

• Gifted services are determined at the state and local level. With a focus on general student proficiency—marked by the emphasis on state-wide achievement tests—not much money is allocated for gifted programs. Gifted education is often an afterthought for many schools. Only four of the 32 states that provide money for gifted programs fully fund the needs of their students. As a result, many gifted programs run on very small budgets and have limited resources.

• There is a lot of debate in the field as to how gifted children are identified. Most of the time, a child is initially identified as having the potential to be gifted by an elementary school teacher, based primarily on their school performance. Once they are acknowledged as possibly gifted, they are administered some form of standardized testing. This can be problematic for a variety of reasons. First, general education teachers may not be adequately equipped to recognize gifted students. Furthermore, a test score may not be a good indicator of giftedness. Intelligence is a wide-ranging variable. Depending on the testing used, it may not encompass all facets of intelligence. Moreover, there are many who believe that standardized tests of intelligence favor the wealthy, because they have had opportunities and experiences that poorer children have not.

• Giftedness as a construct is problematic, because it is likely neither static or dichotomic. If testing occurs in second grade, who is to say that same student would still be considered gifted a few years later? What about those students that miss the cutoff by a point or two? They may be gifted but could have had a bad day during testing. Once a child is labeled as gifted or non-gifted, it is difficult to change that label at a later time. Additionally, why is being gifted an all-or-nothing proposition? Is having a cutoff line based on a standardized test a fair assessment of whether a student is truly gifted? As you can see, the labeling of children as gifted is fraught with problems. It is why some educators, such as James Borland, have called for the label of giftedness to be abolished.

• The socioeconomic and racial disparity in gifted programs is probably the most controversial issue in gifted education. The National Association for Gifted Children notes that African American, Hispanic, and Native American children are underrepresented by at least 50 percent in gifted programs. In a Fordham Institute study, researchers Christopher Yaluma and Adam Tyner found that 12.4 percent of students in wealthier schools take part in gifted programs, but in poor schools, less than half of that number (6.1 percent) participate.

• There are numerous possible reasons for these disparities. First, poorer schools may not have the resources to identify worthy students. Although poorer schools have as many gifted programs as wealthy schools, they may not have the means to accurately identify students. Screening students for gifted programs costs money. Additionally, minority parents of students may not be as knowledgeable about the gifted process and do not nominate their children for gifted services as often."

Clay Cooper, in his article STEM Pros and Cons in the 2020 Prep Expert, dated July 31, 2019, noted, "**STEM programs are often pegged as being elitist towards kids.** STEM programs cater better to students who are naturally motivated and prepared to succeed. As a result, STEM programs often won't cater to lower-achieving students, even though those very same kids could be just as successful as their counterparts with additional help."

In summary, this is not to imply that specialty programs or specialty schools should be abolished. More importantly the point is to be cognizant of the potential pitfalls to providing equity to all students. As often noted, for a myriad of reasons, most of the students in the specialty programs and specialty schools are those from the wealthier families. Secondly, many of the students placed in specialty programs and specialty schools are misplaced. Third, specialty programs and specialty schools require more funding than the normal/comprehensive school. Thus, one of two things generally happens: 1) funds are taken from the normal/comprehensive school to adequately fund the specialty programs or 2) the specialty programs are underfunded.

Again, the major takeaway from this information is insuring equity for all students in these and other programs. To provide equity will require major revision to the current selection process for many/most specialty programs and schools. Even the lottery system for selection falls short on providing the equity for all students.

SEVENTEENTH LETTER
A CALL TO SHARE

SYSTEMIC RACISM IN EDUCATION:
WHY ARE OUR SCHOOLS STILL SEGREGATED?

Theoretically, schools throughout the United States are integrated. It is my contention that the only truth in that statement lies in what's written on paper – nothing more. The reality is that our schools are at best – de-segregated – and in many cases still segregated. First, let's look at the history of school integration (I prefer the term desegregation). According to Wikipedia, The Free Encyclopedia, *School integration in the United States*, "Some schools in the United States were integrated before the mid-20th century, the first ever being Lowell High School in Massachusetts, which has accepted students of all races since its founding. The earliest known African American student, Caroline Van Vronker, attended the school in 1843." As I mentioned in a previous letter, it's important to recall when Africans were brought to America as slaves (1619), it was against the law for them to be taught. Thus, over 225 years after slaves were brought to America, the first school integration took place.

The next important milestone in the "integration of schools" was the post-Civil War era. As pointed out in Wikipedia, "After the Civil War, the first legislation providing rights to African Americans was passed. The 13th, 14th, and 15th Amendments, also known as the Reconstruction Amendments, which were passed between 1865 and 1870, abolished slavery, guaranteed citizenship and protection under the law, and prohibited racial discrimination in voting, respectively." In spite of those actions, Jim Crow laws were established to negate all of that. Thus, segregated schools were maintained. The effect of segregated schools was evident when, 'between 1902 and 1918, the General Education Board, a philanthropic organization created to strengthen public schools in the South, gave only $2.4 million to black schools compared to $25 million given to white schools." Then, "…in a unanimous 1954 decision in the Brown v. Board of Education case, the United States Supreme Court ruled segregation in public schools unconstitutional." Again, there was a mandate to desegregate schools. But did that make it happen, NO. Many states built new schools for whites and blacks to maintain segregation. In South Carolina up to 1960, for example, for black students who wished to go to graduate school, the state paid for them to attend schools in other states rather than admit them to all white universities in the state. It was not until 1957, when the nine black students entered previously all white public schools in Little Rock, Arkansas, that the first desegregation of schools began. That was forced on the system after much resistance. Following that, desegregation started to take place at previously all white universities in the early 1960s; the desegregation of public schools throughout the South followed in the mid-1960s and 1970s.

As I pointed out in an earlier letter, this period of desegregating public schools coincides with the opening of many private and parochial schools – purpose – to maintain segregation (in most cases). This pattern continues today (2020). Private schools are predominantly white. Here's where the issue becomes complex. Follow the logic: 1) parents 'want the best education their child(ren)' so they send them to private school. Some black parents, who can afford it, also 'want the best education their child(ren)' so they send them to private schools. This removes a significant population of students who have opportunities from the public school. That leaves behind a greater proportion of students who do not have opportunity. The biggest hindrance to closing the achievement gap is closing the opportunity gap. The current process with private schools, specialty schools, parochial schools, and home schooling is widening the opportunity gap. Therefore, public schools are set up for failure. Again, in order to close the achievement gap, the opportunity gap must be closed. Oh, by the way, charter schools and school choice IS NOT THE ANSWER. This only widens the opportunity gap. The more the opportunity gap is widened, the higher the failure rate of public schools.

The center of the paradigm above is selfishness, self-centeredness, and an unwillingness to sacrifice. In order for a team to do well, the coach must maximize the team's performance. It is not done by only maximizing a few players' performance – many NFL and NBA teams have learned that lesson the hard way. Education is the same analogy. Many of those students who don't have the opportunities could be the major contributors to the education process and the future of our nation. A rather far-reaching example: suppose the person who has the potential to develop the cure for breast cancer is from a low income home and never gets the opportunity to study at the challenging level to develop her/his potential. Without the opportunity, this person's potential is never realized – thus what could have been, won't be. It may come as a surprise to some, but the kid with the most money/resources is not always the one who has the greatest potential.

Please allow me to give an illustration of the affect it can have when those with resources are in the same school with those without resources. Two students in accelerated classes together – one from an affluent family, the other from a very poor family – in South Carolina. The student from the affluent family has access to an opportunity to spend a summer as part of a Summer Science Institute attending classes at Knoxville College and gaining experience at Oak Ridge National Laboratory. The student from the poor family, because he was in classes with the other student, learned of the opportunity. Both students applied and both students attended the institute. The student from the poor family was ranked the top student in mathematics in his division. Because of this opportunity, he went on to major in mathematics in college, and later be selected to be in charge of a major military program in President Reagan's Star Wars Program managing a $1.3B budget, serve in the military and retire at the rank of colonel, and receive a doctoral degree from George Washington University. It is very unlikely that he would have been able to achieve those things in his life without having the opportunities — starting with the Summer Science Institute. Footnote: the other student from the more affluent family also had a very successful life.

Are schools segregated today and if so, why? According to USA TODAY, *America's segregated schools: We can'0t live together until we learn together*, 23 June 2020, by Stefan Lallinger, "The main reason school districts have been gerrymandered to perpetuate segregation is the tacit, and at times explicit, approval of people of means. Today, nearly one-fifth of public schools have almost no children of color, while another one-fifth have almost no white children. The number of highly segregated nonwhite schools has tripled over the last quarter-century. What's more, predominantly white school districts receive $23 billion more in funding compared with predominantly nonwhite school districts, according to a recent report. This segregation persists despite mountains of evidence demonstrating that students who attend school in integrated settings harbor fewer prejudices and have less discriminatory attitudes."

My challenge is always to see: 1) which adults went to private/parochial schools, 2) whose children are going or went to private/parochial schools, and 3) did they and/or their children go to college. The reason for this information is that many do not acknowledge how private schools, parochial schools, home schooling, and specialty schools all contribute to the perpetuation of segregated schools and racism. This is not unique to white families. Black families with resources also contribute to this perpetuation of racism by sending their children to the private, parochial, and specialty schools.

BOTTOM LINE: To contribute to the elimination of racism, segregated schools, and failing schools, parents with resources must have a change of heart. That change of heart is that, "I will stop my selfish, self-centered, non-sacrificial pattern of being only concerned about providing the best for my child(ren) with little to no consideration of those much less fortunate."

SEND YOUR CHILDREN TO PUBLIC SCHOOLS

Why? This is the avenue to closing the achievement gap. The achievement gap can only be closed by first closing the opportunity gap. As stated previously, potential/ability without opportunity means potential will NEVER be fulfilled. To close the opportunity gap requires providing the resources to ALL, so ALL have the opportunities necessary to achieve. By closing the opportunity gap and the achievement gap, everyone will benefit. We pay a bigger price denying the opportunities than what it costs to provide the opportunity. A large percentage of the prison population is the result of lack of opportunities. "Wealthier communities have less crime and violence than poor communities. This is not because there are more police in the wealthier communities; it's because the wealthier communities have more resources (e.g., activities for children, social outlets, higher level of education, job opportunities, etc....)."

I recognize this is a huge shift that I am suggesting. However, we've got a huge issue to solve, and without solving it, the price we all must pay will continue going up – incarceration, crime, teen pregnancy, dysfunctional communities, and families.

EIGHTEENTH LETTER
A CALL TO SHARE

SYSTEMIC RACISM:

DO WHITES FEEL SUPERIOR

To Other Ethnicities In America?

There is no short or all inclusive answer to this question. However, it is worth exploring the history to find what might be close to an answer. The history for this question reaches much further back than I ever imagined. As reported in Quora, September 12, 2019, "If you truly want to know, the idea of superiority goes back over 34,000 years ago to people who were hunting mammoths in the Eurasian Steppe. The first culture that we know of that was practicing social hierarchy and burying their elite with rich grave goods is found in Sunghir Russia 34,000 years before present." One might quickly say this has no bearing on the question in today's world. Well, as pointed out by The Rev. Dr. William J. Gardiner, in *REFLECTIONS ON THE HISTORY OF WHITE SUPREMACY IN THE UNITED STATES*, March 2009, Elizabeth Martinez in her paper "What is White Supremacy?" defines it in this way, "White Supremacy is a historically based, institutionally perpetuated system of exploitation and oppression of continents, nations, and peoples of color by white peoples and nations of the European continent, for the purpose of maintaining and defending a system of wealth, power, and privilege."

As written in *The Origins of White Supremacy*, by Chelli Stanley, 27 November 2019, "The massacres in Europe lasted at least 500 years. Public tortures, inquisitions. Generation after generation of entire communities forced to watch their family, friends, and neighbors terrorized and killed in front of them."

Wikipedia records, "Charlemagne 782 AD ordered the massacre of 4,500 imprisoned rebel pagan Saxons in response to losing two envoys, four counts, and twenty nobles in battle with the Saxons during his campaign to conquer and Christianize the Saxons during the Saxon Wars. St. Brice's Day massacre was the killing of Danes in the Kingdom of England on Friday, the 13th of November 1002, ordered by King Æthelred the Unready. In response to the frequent Danish raids, King Æthelred ordered the execution of all Danes living in England." This is the major period of massacres of whites.

Stanley continues, "The ideology of white supremacy as we know it came at the end of this specific period of history during which immense traumas occurred simultaneously: the mass killing and public torture of women, the brutal assault against common people, the 'thought-police' Inquisition committees, the terror from which one could almost not escape, and the enslavement of White people throughout the region. This all happened in the centuries before the transatlantic slave trade. Many have wondered how White people came up with the brutal tortures they imposed on Native and African people in 'the Americas.' A look into history shows that many of the same tactics were used on White people during the genocide against them. White people were *intimately familiar* with being enchained themselves , necks in iron, shackled in rows together, taken on ships here and there, sold in markets – for centuries. They were also enslaved throughout the region during the same period as African people, likely side by side, during the Arabic and Viking slave trades that preceded the transatlantic one. In Europe those days, the people who escaped slavery were certainly not free. They were lynched, burned in public executions, tortured at length in public, and hunted down – by the millions."

This is a little publicized phenomenon – that for over 500 years whites endured the same treatment they subsequently imposed on others.

Shortly after they (whites) got from under the tyranny of lynchings and maltreatment, they almost immediately began imposing that treatment on others. This turnabout began as early as the 1100s A.D.

The main takeaway at this point is that the concept of 'white supremacy' has a very long history associated with it. One must recognize that many ideals and cultural mores are rooted in history; therefore, the history oftentimes tends to perpetuate itself without a consciousness that this is the case. For example, the descendants of my father do not argue. I never gave it much thought until I reached adulthood and my wife pointed out to someone that I don't argue. I began exploring that and found that my siblings do not argue among each other. Then it went further that they do not argue (not to be interpreted that they don't disagree). It's that we don't try to convince someone of our point of view when they have demonstrated that they are not open to it. Upon conferring with my siblings, we all agreed that we had never heard our father argue with our mother; and further, we never witnessed him arguing with anyone. The next step was discussing this with our mother. She shared that our father's father (my grandfather, whom I never knew) was a very calm man and not argumentative.

Back to the main point of superiority, we fast forward to centuries later. THE SUN, 8 November 2019, quoted Historian Dr Mary Rambaran-Olm, Canadian historian, "Anglo-Saxon traditionally refers to warring groups from Denmark, Germany and the Netherlands who invaded Britain in the fourth century AD. Historically, the people in early England or 'Englelond' did not call themselves 'Anglo-Saxons.' The term was used sporadically during the early-English period, but by and large the people in early medieval England referred to themselves as 'Englisc' or 'Anglecynn'." Anglo-Saxon became more popular as a phrase in the 18th and 19th centuries when it was used to link white people to their 'supposed origins.' However, more recently the phrase has been adopted by white-supremacists to describe white people of British origin."

As written in Quora, May 21, 2016, "This racism would likely not have taken form if Europe had not experienced a game-changing advancement in technology during the Atlantic slave trade, at a time when east Asia was at the height of its economic wealth. The reason the Europeans were able to profit the most from trade with Asia was its key location in the center of the world, and there was no better way to put this to use than with Europe's unrivaled sea power and ship making. During the 16th century, Europe used its ships to begin to dominate the world when before that, it was less advanced than the Indian and Chinese empires. Because the Chinese and Indians were doing so well, they had no incentive to expand into Europe nor Africa. While the Chinese had little desire to trade, the Indians were more than willing to trade with the Europeans because the Indians had no naval force. So, while the Indians and Chinese were gradually stagnating, the Europeans were able to use their sea power and key geographic location to grow and make huge profit.

Secondly, their dominance of the sea also allowed the Europeans to make inroads in Africa to collect free labor in the form of slaves. The profits from the slave trade were a huge factor in eventually financing the industrial revolution, which allowed the Europeans to get an even faster head start socioeconomically. Slave labor allowed the Americas to dominate the cotton market during a time when Indian cotton was banned in western Europe. When China began to unwittingly use silver as their currency (silver was rare in Asia), they then began to trade with Europe who had a huge supply of it from the Americas. This also led to eventual decline of China as a superpower. During the industrial revolution, China's lack of proximity to coal and iron deposits decelerated its technological advance compared to Europe." Gardiner says, "Any attempt by those of us who are white to deal with issues of white identity must be grounded in an understanding of how white identity came to be shaped over the past four hundred years."

The last bit of information to set the stage for the answer to the subject question – "Do Whites feel superior to other ethnicities in America?" – comes from the book, *White Fragility*, by Robin Diangelo. She points out, "The tension between the noble ideology of equality and the cruel reality of genocide, enslavement, and colonization had to be reconciled.

Thomas Jefferson (who himself owned hundreds of enslaved people) and others turned to science. Jefferson suggested that there were natural differences between the races and asked scientists to find them...Drawing on the work of Europeans before them, American scientists began searching for the answer to the perceived inferiority of non-Anglo groups. Illustrating the power of our questions to shape the knowledge we validate, these scientists didn't ask, 'Are blacks (and others) inferior?' They asked, 'Why are blacks (and others) inferior?' In less than a century, Jefferson's suggestion of racial difference became commonly accepted scientific 'fact.'"

From that point forward, White America has been living with the acceptance that blacks (and others) were inferior. This belief was further perpetuated via Jim Crow laws in the post-Civil War era (1865 – 1964). These laws all placed blacks, Native Americans, and others in a "marginal" category – that is an inferior category. With the advent of radio and television, blacks and Native Americans were generally cast as characters of low intelligence, low-income, and "the bad guys." This characterization was pervasive in practically all segments of the society. One well known show on radio and television that exemplified this characterization was the "Amos and Andy Show." "*Amos 'n' Andy* is an American radio and television sitcom set in Harlem, the historic center of Afro-American culture in New York City. The original radio show, which ran from 1928 to 1960, was created, written and voiced by two white actors." (Wikipedia) This show was riddled with buffoon behavior by the cast (all black). Combined with the portrayal of blacks in marginal roles in the media, in commercials, the white image portrayed good, and the black image portrayed bad or evil. Dolls and figurines were nearly always white. The church adopted some of the same characterizations with "white angels" representing good and "black angels" representing bad and evil. Oh, by the way, there is NO reference to ethnicity of angels in the Bible. For decades, these characterizations were pervasive throughout nearly all aspects of our society.

Since the 1960's, the shift has been from low intellect to thuggish. Generally, when a black youth is seen – the first thought is a negative image. A white youth dressed in the same attire does not receive that same perceived image. That is not to imply that the perception has changed about the intellectual level of blacks being low.

With hundreds of years of programming, whites have developed into the belief of white superiority when compared to blacks, Native American, Latinos….Again, before saying, "Oh, not me," I invite each to do a methodical search deep within and check your findings. This one may take a little time to marinade.

The topic of the next letter: "DO BLACKS FEEL INFERIOR TO OTHER ETHNICITIES IN AMERICA?

NINETEENTH LETTER
A CALL TO SHARE

SYSTEMIC RACISM:

DO BLACKS FEEL INFERIOR

To Other Ethnicities In America?

Part I

I begin this letter with two questions, rather than one. The first question is that posed in the title – do blacks feel inferior to other ethnicities in America? If the answer to the first question is yes, then the second question is why do blacks feel inferior to other ethnicities? Even addressing the first question carries with it assumptions and qualifiers. Because of the implications that may accompany the response, there will likely be a reluctance to answering the question by every ethnicity. In the first segment I will provide some thoughts in response to the first question – do blacks feel inferior to other ethnicities?

One area that may provide some basis for an answer is personal appearance. Why do some blacks bleach their skin to make it lighter? Why do some color their hair? Why do some straighten their hair? Within the black community, changing skin color and artificial hair colors often imply that the person is not happy with their natural appearance and attempt to emulate characteristics of whites.

Sean Cooper, psychologist, notes in his blog on *8 Signs of An Inferiority Complex*, "an inferiority complex usually means you feel incomplete, **unworthy and unacceptable as a person no matter what you do,** achieve or fix about yourself." He goes on to identify the eight signs of an inferiority complex:

1) Perfectionism: To a perfectionist, nothing they do is ever good enough.

2) Submissive Behavior: This theory says that how you act and feel inside are often determined by what you perceive your social status or rank to be.

3) Being Ultra-Sensitive: When you feel inferior, any small critical comment can often send you into a spiral of depression and self-hate for days. Any slight sign of rejection or exclusion will make you feel totally miserable.

4) Procrastination and Inaction: You become so emotionally sensitive to failure that you avoid trying at all.

5) Social Media Triggers Feelings of Guilt, Jealousy Or Shame

6) You're Secretly Very Judgmental of Other People

7) You Try to Hide Your Flaws or Distract People From Them... Without Success

8) Always Comparing Yourself to Another Person's #1 Winning Quality

The signs of an inferiority complex are provided to assist in assessing if inferiority is present. They are not absolutes, but indicators. These signs will not establish the level of inferiority, only if it is present.

There is no scientific answer to the question – Do Blacks Feel Inferior to Other Ethnicities? There are those who would shudder at the thought of a "yes" response to the question; there are some who would be angry; there are some who would be surprised; and, then there are those who would say "yes" is the obvious answer. Regardless of what your response is, I am going to forge on to looking at the reasons *why* "yes" might be the appropriate answer. The other caveat to this is that there are exceptions regardless of the answer.

The why "yes" to this question can come as the result of many factors: 1) history/education, 2) experiences, 3) culture, 4) media, 5) programming, 6) laws, 7) economics, 8) religion/the church, and others (this list is by no means all inclusive). As I look at these factors, I quickly realize that I cannot cover all in one letter. Therefore, we will begin this letter with the discussion on History and Education.

I. History and Education:

Nairaland Forum, Dr Bedford Umez's presentation, *Blacks Are Educated to Feel Inferior,* February 1, 2013, "Black people are actually covertly being taught to believe that they are inferior mostly through the use of mass media. There is a document, called *d mandate dat*, which was supposedly given to all of the first African missionaries of the 1890s, and it in synopsis states:

1. Teach them (Africans) to read and not to reason.

2. Teach them to focus and keep 'lookin unto the sky and neva into d ground'

3. Teach them to believe in a supreme God and not their gods..."

We have previously covered much of the historical perspective. So briefly, the history goes back to the days of missionaries as early as the 12th Century going into Africa. Their approach was as described by Dr. Umez above. Because the Africans wore little clothing, they were viewed as uncivilized; because they didn't communicate the way the missionaries did, they were uncivilized; because they didn't read and write, they were uncivilized; because their cuisine was not the same as the missionaries, they were uncivilized; and because their belief system was not the same, they were uncivilized. Note the pattern, if they are not like us, then they are uncivilized. That set of assumptions has been the modus operandi for every exploration going to a new land. Let it be clear – that is a false and faulty set of assumptions. That was the set of assumptions that went along with the exploration to America. The Native Americans were not "like us;" therefore, they were uncivilized, wild people. One of the first actions of the discoverers of the new world (America) was to enlist the Native Americans as servants. The next major indicator of placing the

Native Americans in an "inferior" status was declaring that they were NOT citizens when the colonist drew up documents outlining citizenship. A pure slap in the face when the Native Americans were in America before the colonists arrived.

Then we move forward to the importation of slaves (blacks from Africa). The slaves were looked upon and treated as sub-human. As described in Wikipedia, "To ensure profitability, the owners of the ships divided their hulls into holds with little headroom, so they could transport as many slaves as possible. Unhygienic conditions, dehydration, dysentery and scurvy led to a high mortality rate, on average 15% and up to a third of captives. Often the ships carried hundreds of slaves, who were chained tightly to plank beds. For example, the slave ship *Henrietta Marie* carried about 200 slaves on the long Middle Passage. They were confined to cargo holds with each slave chained with little room to move."

After freeing of the slaves (1865), whites continued treating blacks as sub-humans during what was known as the Jim Crow era (1865 – 1964). Thus the history serves as an influence to feeling inferior today. The League for the Fifth International article, *"The Oppression of Black People in the USA Today*, February 10, 2008, summarizes the history this way, "The systematic oppression of black Americans is deeply embedded in the fabric of US society. In a nation made up of immigrants, blacks were the ones brought there forcibly and kept as slaves for 150 years. Although racism afflicts many ethnic groups, racism against black people is "justified" by a racist ideology derived from slavery and the hundred year old apartheid system of Jim Crow, which insists on their inferiority to whites. Though officially hidden today, it underpins the horrific inequality in education, employment, housing, healthcare, and levels of poverty dividing black and white Americans."

During the era of slavery (legalized slavery), one of the keys to maintain the slaves was to deny the opportunity to learn – including reading and writing. It was realized very early that education is power. One of the ways to keep a people powerless is to keep them in ignorance. Thus, they are dependent on those who are educated and consequently those with power. As we study history, we see that those blacks who were able to get educated made significant changes in their lives and oftentimes in the lives of others.

During the Jim Crow era – following the era of slavery – education continued to be used as a tool to keep blacks from gaining power. Even when schools were provided, they were poorly equipped. During the 1940s many of the black teachers were only educated to the eighth-grade level. In many of the southern states where the black colleges did not have a masters' degree program, if a black person wanted to attend graduate school, the state would pay all expenses for that student to attend a northern college. That technique also limited the number of blacks who would go on to get advance degrees. This was not a publicized policy therefore a black would have to apply to the white college, then when rejected, must apply to a northern college. If accepted to the northern college and they pursued their request to the state, then the state would pay for them to attend the northern college. This was another technique of suppression in the area of education.

In the late 1950s and early 1960s, federal grants assisted the states with maintaining segregation by providing programs to the black colleges (e.g., law school, medical schools, agriculture, nursing, and home economics). This continued until the early 1970s. At that point the black colleges (known as HBCUs – Historically Black Colleges and Universities) were thriving with growing and productive student bodies. As previously stated, each time there is significant progress being made toward equality, steps are taken to retard the progress. In this case, states (especially southern states) began withdrawing support for some of the programs in HBCUs and limiting the program to the predominantly white universities (e.g., law program, agriculture, nursing, home economics, and engineering). Black schools were beginning to provide a large number of qualified people in these professions by the mid-1980s. With the withdrawal of support came the legislative action with state supported black universities to eliminate the programs. The impact of this was the decline in enrollment at HBCUs. The decline in enrollment then justified the further reduction in funding. It became a catch-22 for many of HBCUs.

Simultaneously with the decrease funding for HBCUs was the repeal of affirmative action. In many circles the repeal of affirmative action was morally justified by hiring non-competitive blacks into positions to show 'we have blacks in our organization.' At the highest level, this was done with the appointment of Clarence Thomas to the US Supreme Court. The other argument for the repeal of affirmative action was that this was discriminating by denying the positions to qualified persons of other ethnicities. Well, glory be! The discrimination was ok for hundreds of years to blacks, but now it was not ok to allow blacks to catch up for the years left behind. You see, if there is nothing implemented to allow the catch up, then the catching up will never take place. In a 26-mile race, those that you are racing against start the race 10 to 15 miles ahead. Running as fast as you can against those who are that far ahead makes it nearly impossible to catch them – especially when they don't stop running.

The next letter will pick up with
The Impact that Experience and Culture have on Inferiority

TWENTIETH LETTER
A CALL TO SHARE

SYSTEMIC RACISM:

DO BLACKS FEEL INFERIOR

To Other Ethnicities In America?

Part Ii: Inferiority Continued

We will continue addressing reasons why Blacks might feel inferior. As we transition among the reasons, keep in mind the signs of inferiority outlined in Part I. The next section on Culture and Experiences is closely related to History and Education. Many of the areas from culture make the history, so do our experiences. The Culture and Experiences segment is more personal.

I. Culture and Experiences:

A recent study from the Pew Research Center, April 2, 2015, suggests that subconscious preferences for different racial groups persist, even among multiracial adults. Researchers at the Pew Research Center say that "most humans display a bias against out-groups—people who are different from them," and a team of researchers wanted to find out whether biracial adults were less likely to have implicit racial biases because of their multicultural backgrounds. Pew says that the study's findings suggest that biracial adults are "simply more divided in their racial preferences."

Subconscious racial preferences can alter behavior, according to the Pew Research Center, "A 2007 study conducted by Harvard Medical

School found that white doctors with high levels of implicit bias against blacks were less likely to treat black patients."

The attitude by many blacks toward school has had a major impact on the culture – particularly in the black community. The belief that blacks and school don't go together has its roots in slavery's refusal to let blacks be educated. But it gained strength in the mid-1960s. This created an experience among young blacks of inferiority and attacking it in negative ways. John H. McWhorter, in his article, *What's Holding Blacks Back?* in the City Journal, 2001, describes this experiential phenomenon, "The 'acting white' charge—which implies that you think yourself different from, and better than, your peers—is the prime reason that blacks do poorly in school. The gifted black student quickly faces a choice between peer group acceptance and intellectual achievement. Most, out of an utterly human impulse, choose the former (peer group acceptance). Even if they open themselves to schooling in college or later, their performance all too often permanently suffers from the message they long ago internalized that 'the school thing' is an add-on, not a mix-in."

There are a few highlights from my experience that were like a common thread in the lives of many blacks during the 50s, 60s and 70s. One of those was being told, 'you have to be better than them to compete with them.' A prime example that went along with that was Jackie Robinson's entrance into Major League Baseball. As noted in Daily History.org, 22 November 2018, "Jackie Robinson was the first African American to play in major league baseball on April 15, 1947. The United States was still legally segregated throughout the south and tradition and custom segregated much of the rest of the country. The armed forces were still segregated by race and the national pastime, baseball, was as well. The idea that any of these laws, customs or institutions would change was almost impossible to fathom. Yet, Jackie Robinson would not only integrate baseball that spring, but by the fall of 1947 he would play in the World Series and was named the Rookie of the Year for the season." He had to be so much better than them to be considered for competing with them.

The motto at my high school (an all-black school in the 50s and 60s) was "strive to excel; not to equal." Somehow, we tied those two together as marching orders for what it took for a black person to be successful in America. So regardless of what it was, you had to be better in order to be equal.

Jim Crow laws made it a necessity for black parents to have 'the talk' with their children in the era of 1865 to 1964. But then with the advent of the Civil Rights Act of 1964, the written laws enforcing racism were abolished. As we learned in very short order, the laws were abolished; however, the racism set forth in the laws remained. Thus, it became less obvious of the requirement for the talk. Many families instituted or continued the talk, while others did not know of the unwritten requirement until, in many cases, they experienced it firsthand — oftentimes resulting in loss of a loved one, imprisonment, cost in money or property, or some other form of paying the penalty for not staying in their place.

Black girls had the experience of having the beauty standards all based on white people. This included the attitude that the lighter your complexion the prettier you were. Therefore, a dark-skinned black girl was ALWAYS ugly. The easier your hair was to comb, the better your hair was. The smaller your lips were, the prettier your face was. And that list goes on to the extent that a white girl was always prettier than a black girl. Thus, the foundation of inferiority based on beauty.

In Ivy Panda, an academic editing hub: Free Study Hub, January 13, 2020, essay *Barbie Dolls: Positive and Negative Impacts on Children*, "Barbie is one of the oldest toys in the United States. It was created by Ruth Handler in the year 1959. Ruth's main intention behind creating Barbie was to craft a character that his daughter could look up to as a model of inspiration. As a business model, Barbie was the roles they play in setting the racial bias. There was a very long period of time when black intended to be an upbeat model for the juvenile girls. But unfortunately, due to various allegations and finger pointing, this particular intention was defeated." Although the founder had good intentions, the results have been negatively impacting in many ways. The Barbie Doll has, unfortunately provided a role model for young girls leading to low self-esteem and eating disorders. In a Huffpost article, *The New Diversity in Barbie Dolls: Radical Change or More of the Same*, February 7, 2017, Julie Wosk reports, "According to some calculations, the typical 11.5" Barbie represents a woman whose figure measurements are 38-18-34—a tough goal for young women to attain. With their idealized adult female bodies and their perky pretty faces, Barbies have long been versions of the Perfect Woman—a paradigm, largely created by men that has haunted women for centuries and continues to worry parents whose daughters may fret about their own imperfect figures. Critics for years have been complaining that Barbie is a bad cultural model for young girls to mirror or imitate.

Mattel introduced its first African American and Latina Barbies in 1980, but researchers Derek Hopson and Darlene Powell Hopson in their 1990 book, *Different and Wonderful,* reported that black children preferred white dolls over black dolls, indicating that the children had self-esteem issues. The authors urged parents to help change their children's perceptions and also buy their children black Barbies because, as the Hopsons emphasized with italics, "*You do not want your child to grow up thinking that only White dolls and by extension White people are attractive and nice.*"

I used the illustration of the impact of Barbie Dolls on the culture to highlight what effect a multiplicity of actions have and parents could not find any toys for their children who looked like them. In the 100 Black Men of America, their motto is, "What they see is what they'll be." This is an impactful statement. What kids see as they are growing up plays a strong role on the development of their self-image.

For today's black adults (primarily over 50 years old), many can cite having at least one of the following experiences in their lifetime:

1. Applying for a position and finding out a white person, who is less qualified, was hired and oftentimes is a relative of someone in a supervisory or executive position.

2. A white person wanting to touch your skin or hair out of curiosity about how it feels.

3. Being seen in a classy home, car, gathering, or attire and the assumption being made that you are "the help" – butler, maid, servant, or attendant).

4. Being the senior executive in a group with whites and others not knowing the group continuously turning to a subordinate of theirs for information or direction rather than the black senior executive.

5. Being told by a taxi driver that he or she cannot take you to "that neighborhood."

6. Getting on an elevator and white person(s) on the elevator shift away from you.

7. Being questioned if you can afford an item (e.g., clothing, car, etc....)

8. Being told, "You are very articulate." (Implying you are not expected to be articulate).

9. Attending a company social function or corporate level conference and being the only black present.

10. Being followed by the security person in a clothing or department store.

11. Being stopped by the police and told you were stopped because of a report of a stolen car.

12. Being assigned the additional duty in the company as sports activities coordinator or the Equal Opportunity representative.

13. Being guided toward a profession more focused on manual labor rather than science, math, engineering, or technology.

14. A professional black female being referred to as aggressive.

15. The assumption that a black person can dance, play sports, and eats fried chicken.

I am certain that the above list is not all inclusive of the experience blacks have encountered which imply that they are inferior. Oftentimes when in conversation with white persons, when they talk about another black person, that person was a cook, maid, custodian, etc. This indicates that their primary interaction with blacks have been those in the mentioned positions. This is also an indicator of the image that person holds of blacks.

Being guilty of any of the above would not automatically label an individual as racist – in the average interpretation of the word. However, it does point out the presence of systemic racism embedded in the culture. If one's response is that these are minor, then it indicates a lack of understanding and recognition that these are not isolated occurrences. I have personally experienced 12 of the 15 examples listed above. In addition, each of the 12 have occurred multiple times.

A long-standing technique for promoting inferiority is the Fear Factor. To get higher prices in the sale of slaves, the strength, virility, rough/tough images were the major marketing tools. The Jim Crow era (1865 to 1960) was marked with the fear factors of stealing, lazy, ignorant and other descriptors portraying blacks as a threat to the society. From the early 1960 thru the present, the fear factors have been blacks are a threat to the safety of the "citizens" (whites). During the Civil Rights era (1960 to 1975), the fear factors included: 1) they (blacks) want to take your jobs; 2) they want to go to your schools and your (White) children will not be able to get the quality of education they use to get; 3) they (blacks) want to marry your white daughters; and 4) they (blacks) want to move into your (white) neighborhoods and that will lower your property value. All those things incited the white population (particularly the white males). The current era, which began in the late 70s, incites fear in whites by portraying blacks as thugs, rioters, looters, and radicals. Today, as throughout the history of blacks in America, blacks are portrayed as a threat to society and the physical well-being of its citizens (whites). The amazing thing is that this theme has been used for 400 years and it is still effective in influencing the thoughts, actions, and behaviors of a significant percentage of whites. This is very evident as you watch political commercials over the last ten years. Political commercials against a black or someone supportive of racial equality continue to focus on that person being a threat to the perceived way of life enjoyed by middle and higher class whites in the 1950s. This process has gone so long that it is embedded in the culture.

One might ask, "Well, how do we change these behaviors in our culture?" My first and immediate response would be, "I'm glad you asked." Then we could proceed with suggestions taken from Robin Diangelo's book, *White Fragility: Why It's So Hard for White People to Talk about Racism*, "Racial stress results from an interruption to the racially familiar. These interruptions can take a variety of forms and come from a range of sources, including:

1. An openness to the suggestion that a white person's viewpoint comes from a racialized frame of reference.

2. People of color talking directly about their own racial perspectives (challenge to white taboos on talking openly about race).

3. People of color choosing not to protect white people's feelings about race.

4. A fellow white disagreeing with 'our' racial beliefs (challenge to white solidarity).

5. Receiving feedback that our behavior had a racist impact (challenge to white racial innocence).

6. An acknowledgment that access is unequal between racial groups (challenge to meritocracy).

7. Being presented with a person of color in a position of leadership (challenge to white authority).

8. Being presented with information about other racial groups through, for example, movies in which people of color drive the action but are not in stereotypical roles, or multicultural education (challenge to white centrality).

9. Suggesting that white people do not represent or speak for all of humanity (challenge to universalism)."

To change a culture requires bold actions on the part of all. It has been said – and I paraphrase – racism will only cease to exist when those who are not affected by it or who profit from it take it just as seriously as those who are.

TWENTY-FIRST LETTER
A CALL TO SHARE

SYSTEMIC RACISM:

DO BLACKS FEEL INFERIOR TO OTHER ETHNICITIES IN AMERICA?

Part III: INFERIORITY CONTINUED MEDIA, PROGRAMMING & LAWS

I. Media:

Charles Love in the New York Post article, *What 'woke' whites get wrong about blacks' priorities*, June 28, 2020, stated, "The media give a distorted view of black life. We see this in the stories they choose to report — and those they eschew. In 2018, police shot and killed 54 unarmed men; 22 were black. Compared with the percentage of blacks in the US population, that figure looks disproportionate — but black people commit a disproportionate amount of violent crime and thus tend to have more interactions with the police. Every police shooting must be investigated thoroughly and fairly, but we should also demand fair and thorough media coverage of these shootings.

Blacks do lag whites in many socioeconomic indicators — but most blacks don't live in poverty, don't have constant run-ins with law enforcement and aren't uneducated. It's important to look at racial disparities in context. Though blacks commit more violent crime than whites do in relative terms, in absolute terms, the percentage of people who commit any violent crime is tiny. The white violent crime rate is 0.12 percent; for blacks, it is 0.44 percent. By any standard, most people aren't violent criminals, regardless of their race. Yet sympathetic non-blacks often see blacks as oppressed victims with limited opportunities."

Love continues, "Since they don't have many blacks in their social circles, and having conversations with blacks is awkward and can take time, woke whites opt for easy, feel-good actions, most of which will have no effect on police brutality, on the quality of black schools or neighborhoods or on black lives generally. Most woke whites have good intentions, but their symbolic gestures will, at best, have little effect and, at worst, do real harm. The campaign against police is a good example. Broad anti-police sentiment has already caused cops to become less proactive in high-crime neighborhoods, with the predictable result that shootings have spiked around the country.

Whites are engaging in activism motivated by a misperception about black life that doesn't comport with reality for most blacks. With their views of blacks as wounded and perpetually oppressed, woke whites would do more good by doing nothing."

One area many may not pay much attention to is the impact the media has on young developing minds. The media is a major source of input to the behavior development of young minds. The Center for Disease Control (CDC) addresses this as Adverse Childhood Experience (ACE). In the CDC Review, 5 November 2019, it states, "Adverse Childhood Experiences (ACEs) are potentially traumatic events that occur in childhood. ACEs can include violence, abuse, and growing up in a family with mental health or substance use problems. Toxic stress from ACEs can change brain development and affect how the body responds to stress. ACEs are linked to chronic health problems, mental illness, and substance misuse in adulthood." The focus on violence and abuse in the media contribute significantly to the behavior outcomes of youth. CDC further found, "1) 61% of adults had at least one ACE and 16% had 4 or more types of ACEs. 2)Females and several racial/ethnic minority groups were at greater risk for experiencing 4 or more ACEs. 3)Many people do not realize that exposure to ACEs is associated with increased risk for health problems across the lifespan.

These things often make up the "Breaking News" on news shows. The majority of primetime TV centers on violence or trauma. For youth who are fortunate enough to live in neighborhoods that do not have violence, the media exposure oftentimes paint a picture of the world beyond their neighborhoods. Thus, creating what might be called a secondary experience, similar to the effect of secondary smoke. The CDC Review points out some things to help prevent the negative impact of these experiences: "1) Reduce stigma around seeking help with parenting challenges or for substance misuse, depression, or suicidal thoughts. 2) Promote safe, stable, nurturing relationships and environments where children live, learn, and play." Reflect on the impact the media could have if the focus was on the two preventative measures listed above. There appears to be this thought that danger, violence, severe trauma, and other things like these are what it takes to get good ratings and viewers. The stronger influence is with positive influences rather than negative ones. Between video games and the proliferation of guns - "the mighty 2nd amendment" - the streets, nightclubs, and even shopping malls are becoming like the wild, wild west. The way that this contributes to Blacks feeling inferior is the thuggish portrayal – some real and some unreal.

II. Programming

The theory that blacks are intellectually inferior to whites and other ethnic groups is one that began centuries ago and continues to surface to this day. Irene Monroe, a religion columnist in her commentary, *Theory of Blacks' Intellectual Inferiority Rears Ugly Head* at Harvard, May 25, 2011, on Boston Public Radio, reported, "The myth of genetic inferiority of people of African ancestry is centuries old, tracing back to when the first slave boat arrived on our shores in 1619 in Jamestown, Virginia. The myth of genetic inferiority of people of African ancestry not only legitimatized slavery, but also biblically sanctioned it. It was aided by people like Nobel Laureate William Shockley, who in 1956 voiced his theory of a genetic basis for racial inferiority. As part of his theory on the biology of ethnicity, Shockley stated that people of African ancestry belonged to a lower species of humanity, and deserved sterilization.

The idea of sterilizing blacks — because we supposedly belonged to a "lower species of humanity" — was part and parcel of the American eugenics movement, which started in 1926. Even Planned Parenthood's founder, Margaret Sanger — an iconic figure for the women's reproductive rights movement — espoused eugenics theory, backing the 1939 "Negro Project," which was a precursor to what eugenists wanted to implement on a much larger scale.

Stephanie Grace, a student editor for the Harvard Law Review, penned an article in the May 26, 2010 issue, "blacks might be genetically inferior to whites I absolutely do not rule out the possibility that African Americans are, on average, genetically predisposed to be less intelligent."

There are numerous stereotypes which contribute to the programming aspect of inferiority. I will list only some of the many: 1) sambo, 2) savagery, 3) mammy, 4) Aunt Jemimah, 5) Sapphire, 6) Jezebelle, 7) violence (as a way of life), 8) welfare mother, and 9) thugs. Although these stereotypes are not used today, they have been replaced by a different set of stereotypes carrying the same messages as earlier. As reported in the Jim Crow Museum Publication, 2020, Laura Green, Virginia Commonwealth University, in her article *Negative Racial Stereotypes and Their Effect on Attitudes Toward African Americans* states, "Although much has changed since the days of Sambo, Jim Crow, the Savage, Mammy, Aunt Jemimah, Sapphire and Jezebelle, it can be argued convincingly that similar stereotypes of African Americans exist in 1998. However, the predominant modern stereotypes are the violent, brutish African American male and the dominant, lazy African American female - the Welfare Mother (Peffley Hurwitz & Sniderman, 1997). Recent research has shown that whites are likely to hold these stereotypes especially with respect to issues of crime and welfare. As political and legislative decisions still are controlled by white males, these negative biases are often expressed through policy formation. There is an obvious trend in this society to discriminate against and deny access to social institutions to African Americans (Jewell, 1993). A 1997 study conducted by Peffley et al indicated that whites who hold negative stereotypes of African Americans judge them more harshly than they do other whites when making hypothetical decisions about violent crimes and welfare benefits."

The programming aspect takes place with both whites and blacks. This is a societal issue. The programming portrays whites, blacks, native Americans, Hispanics, and Asians in stereotypical ways that gets embedded in the minds of all.

III. Laws

The United States of America has a history of using laws to discriminate against minorities. Two of the best-known examples are laws enacted for the benefit of white Americans and in many cases the death of Native Americans. According to the Center for American Progress article by Danyelle Solomon, et.al., *Systemic Inequality: Displacement, Exclusion, and Segregation,* August 7, 2019, "Although American public policies had intentionally displaced people of color for centuries prior, two of the most well-known examples are the Indian Removal Act and the Dawes Act. President Andrew Jackson signed the Indian Removal Act into law in 1830, authorizing the federal government to forcibly relocate Native Americans in the southeast in order to make room for white settlement. For the next two decades, thousands of Native Americans died of hunger, disease, and exhaustion on a forced march west of the Mississippi River—a march now known as the "Trail of Tears." Decades later, in 1887, President Grover Cleveland signed into law the General Allotment Act—better known as the Dawes Act. The Dawes Act forcibly converted communally held tribal lands into small, individually owned lots. The federal government then seized two-thirds of reservation lands and redistributed the land to white Americans. Native American families who were allotted land were encouraged to take up agriculture despite the fact that much of the land was unsuitable for farming and many could not afford the equipment, livestock, and other supplies necessary for a successful enterprise. The result was the erosion of tribal traditions, the displacement of thousands of families, and the loss of 90 million acres of valuable land."

Following the end of the Civil War, 1865, laws — sometimes called 'The Black Codes' or 'Black Laws' were put in place to continue the theory/belief of the inferiority (sub-humanization) of blacks. As recorded in Wikipedia, "The best known of them (Black Laws) were passed in 1865 and 1866 by Southern states, after the American Civil War, in order to restrict African Americans' freedom, and to compel them to work for low wages. Before the war, Northern states that had prohibited slavery also enacted laws similar to the slave codes and the later Black Codes: Connecticut, Ohio, Illinois, Indiana, Michigan, and New York enacted laws to discourage free blacks from residing in those states. They were denied equal political rights, including the right to vote, the right to attend public schools, and the right to equal treatment under the law."

In the Rockaway Youth Task Force publication of 2014, Milan Taylor penned the article, *What Black Rights Mean in the 21st Century*, sharing, "As Michelle Alexander eloquently explains in *The New Jim Crow,* a contemporary racial hierarchy has been formed to congeal longstanding racial injustice. Instead of overt and brutal means to enforce racist social control (such as slavery and Jim Crow), white racist elites have created a criminal justice system buttressed on enduring racial tensions (e.g., Stand Your Ground Law). Today's criminal justice system encapsulates the explosive and dangerous development of private prisons, and expounds upon racist and prejudicial laws meant to oppress, marginalize, and disenfranchise low-income people of color." Note that 'Stand Your Ground Law is defined: "a law that allows citizens to protect themselves if they feel their lives are in danger, regardless of whether they could have safely exited the situation. For example, Stand Your Ground law states that no one should feel forced to leave a premises they have every right to be in." (Legal Dictionary, April 2, 2019) It should not take a rocket scientist to connect the dots on legalizing shooting someone in your neighborhood who is a "thug". And who is the 'thug' or perceived to be thugs? – Black males. So, what's the outcome of this law – Trevon Martin, a 17-year-old youth, killed on his way home in the residential area in 2012. Fast forward to 2020, Ahmaud Arbrey, 25-year-old, confronted, shot and killed while running (in daylight) in his neighborhood. By the way, both of these young men were Black and unarmed.

Two studies published by the American Psychological Association (APA), in 2014 and 2017, found "that black boys as young as 10 may not be viewed in the same light of childhood innocence as their white peers, but are instead more likely to be mistaken as older, be perceived as guilty and face police violence if accused of a crime. With the average age over-estimation for black boys exceeding four-and-a-half years, in some cases, black children may be viewed as adults when they are just 13 years old." (2014) The second study reported, "People See Black Men as Larger, More Threatening, Than Same-Sized White Men, it was revealed that people have a tendency to perceive black men as larger and more threat-ening than similarly sized white men. Unarmed black men are dispropor-tionately more likely to be shot and killed by police, and often these killings are accompanied by explanations that cite the physical size of the person shot." (2017)

In each of the three areas addressed in this letter, we must recognize that within our culture there is a very deeply rooted belief that Blacks are less than. It is constantly evident in the media and laws that are put forth. After it is recognized, then there must be the commitment to have it in the forefront of all phases of our very existence. This is not a committee assignment – this belongs to the entire population, especially the white population. Again, if racism is to be eliminated, then those who are not affected by it or who profit from it must be as committed to eliminating it as those who are affected.

TWENTY-SECOND LETTER
A CALL TO SHARE

SYSTEMIC RACISM:
DO BLACKS FEEL INFERIOR
TO OTHER ETHNICITIES IN AMERICA?
Part III: INFERIORITY CONTINUED ECONOMICS

I. Economics

Enterprise Magazine article, *African American Economics: Real Facts*, March 6, 2019, presents a good picture of the economic situation of Blacks in America. It states, "Some 84% believe the American Dream means financial security; 78% in not living paycheck-to-paycheck; and 77% in owning a home. Yet, based on a new *State of the American Family Study* by Massachusetts Mutual Life Insurance Co. (MassMutual), many African Americans don't have tangible assets needed to make those goals happen now. The study revealed a disconnect between African Americans' financial situations and their hope toward the future. The report disclosed some pitfalls tied to African Americans' personal finances including high debt, low savings, and a lower likelihood of wide financial product ownership. In turn, the financial disparities and the wealth gap possibly explain why 31% surveyed are convinced the American Dream may be fading away.

Some key findings from the survey:

• Outside of retirement accounts, only 37% of African Americans own wealth-building products such as stocks and mutual funds.

• Only 35% believe they are doing a good job of preparing for retirement.

• 33% have less than one month of funds saved for a crisis and less than 25% have amassed more than six months' of emergency savings.

• 58% are actively involved in educating their children on finances versus 48% of Caucasians. Forty percent rely on family members for information.

The study shows African Americans want to improve their financial situations and are hopeful about the future. At the same time, it sheds light on the financial struggles and inequities that the African American community continues to battle."

This addresses the state of blacks in the area of economics. Some consideration must be given to why are blacks in that economic state. The economic story begins in 1619 when Africans were brought to America as slaves. They were brought with only the scanty clothing that they wore. From 1619 to 1865, they worked and received no pay (as slaves). When freed, blacks remained segregated from 1865 to 1965. Although gaining legal civil rights at that point, blacks were not placed on the path to gain a seat in the board room. Without seats in the board room, the trickle-down effect is that there is not an equal proportion of blacks at the supervisory, management, or administrative levels in organizations. Yes, the unemployment percentages may decrease, but the wealth level does not. From the period 1970 to today, blacks are still not approaching the point of having the proportionate quantity of blacks in positions at those levels in organizations.

According to the website: https://blackthen.com/8-successful-and-triving-black-communities-destroyed-by-racist-white-neighbors/, there were eras in which black businesses were thriving. The first one cited was the late 1800s up to 1906 in Atlanta, Georgia. "When the Civil War ended, African Americans in Atlanta began entering the realm of politics, establishing businesses and gaining notoriety as a social class. Increasing tensions between Black wageworkers and the white elite began to grow,

127

and ill-feelings were further exacerbated when Blacks gained more civil rights, including the right to vote. The tensions exploded during the gubernatorial election of 1906 in which M. Hoke Smith and Clark Howell competed for the Democratic nomination. On Sept. 22, 1906, Atlanta newspapers reported four alleged assaults on local white women. Soon, some 10,000 white men and boys began gathering, beating, and stabbing Blacks. It is estimated that there were between 25 and 40 African American deaths; it was confirmed that there were only two white deaths." This was the first of many efforts to disenfranchise African Americans as business owners and building wealth.

Another area which was recognized as an economic boom for African Americans was Tulsa, Oklahoma. The Black Then website reported, "During the oil boom of the 1910s, the area of northeast Oklahoma around Tulsa flourished, including the Greenwood neighborhood, which came to be known as 'the Black Wall Street.'" The area was home to several lawyers, realtors, doctors, and prominent black Businessmen, many of them multimillionaires.

Greenwood boasted a variety of thriving businesses such as grocery stores, clothing stores, barbershops, banks, hotels, cafes, movie theaters, two newspapers, and many contemporary homes. Greenwood residents enjoyed many luxuries that their white neighbors did not, including indoor plumbing and a remarkable school system. The dollar circulated 36 to 100 times, sometimes taking a year for currency to leave the community.

The neighborhood was destroyed during a riot that broke out after a group of men from Greenwood attempted to protect a young Black man from a lynch mob. On the night of May 31, 1921, a mob called for the lynching of Dick Rowland, a Black man who shined shoes, after reports spread that, on the previous day, he had assaulted Sarah Page, a white woman, in the elevator she operated in a downtown building.

In the early morning hours of June 1, 1921, Black Tulsa was looted, firebombed from the air and burned down by white rioters. The governor declared martial law, and National Guard troops arrived in Tulsa. In the wake of the violence, 35 city blocks lay in charred ruins, over 800 people were treated for injuries and estimated 300 deaths occurred."

In a December 26, 2020, New York Times article by Brent Staples, *The Haunting of Tulsa, Okla.,* Staples reports, "The Tulsa, Okla., police department set the stage for mass murder in the spring of 1921 when it deputized members of a mob that invaded and destroyed the prosperous Black enclave of Greenwood. The armed marauders who swept into the community in the early hours of June 1 wreaked havoc in the spirit of a police directive that urged white Tulsans to "Get a gun, and get busy and try to get a nigger."

They murdered at will while forcing Black families from their homes. They looted valuables that included jewelry, furs, and fine furnishings. They used torches and oil-soaked rags to set fires that incinerated homes, churches, doctors' offices, hotels, and other businesses across an area of 35 square blocks. Two months ago, an archaeological team unearthed a mass grave in Tulsa that may answer questions that have troubled the city's sleep for a century. The fact that burial workers installed stairs in the trench suggests that there were quite a few dead to move."

Many other towns saw black-owned businesses beginning to increase and grow. In large cities where the African American population was growing (such as Chicago, New York, Detroit, St. Louis, et.al...), not only were black-owned businesses beginning to flourish, but African Americans were beginning to prosper from wage earning jobs in factories and other businesses. In these cities as Black employment grew, whites began to feel that they were being displaced by Blacks. As cited on the Black Then website, "During spring 1917 Blacks were arriving in St. Louis at the rate of 2,000 per week, with many of them finding work at the Aluminum Ore Company and the American Steel Company in East St. Louis.

Some whites feared loss of job and wage security because of the new competition, and further resented newcomers arriving from a rural, very different culture. Tensions between the groups ran high and escalated when rumors were spread about Black men and white women socializing at labor meetings. In May, 3,000 white men gathered in downtown East St. Louis. The roving mob began burning buildings and attacking Black people...Then on July 1st, white men driving a car through a Black neighborhood began shooting into houses, stores, and a church. After the riot, varying estimates of the death toll circulated. The police chief estimated that 100 Blacks had been killed. The renowned journalist Ida B. Wells reported in *The Chicago Defender* that 40-150 black people were killed in the rioting. The NAACP estimated deaths at 100-200. Six thousand African Americans were left homeless after their neighborhood was burned."

These atrocities are not forgotten and cannot be overlooked as we talk about the economic status of Blacks in America. This expulsion wasn't a bizarre anomaly in one part of the country. Between the 1860s and the 1920s, white Americans drove thousands of black residents from their communities. Those who were land and homeowners lost all they had. The homes and land were taken over by whites. One hundred years later (2020), there has been no restitution for those losses. The comment is often made - "Get over it" (with reference to the past that Blacks have endured), or "I didn't commit those atrocities you are talking about," or "Look what 'so and so' has achieved — you can do the same." I often wonder what the outcomes would have been had Black Wall Street in Tulsa not been destroyed but continued to prosper. What would the outcome have been if black businesses which were thriving in the 40s, 50s and early 60s had continued to grow? Would those and other businesses have grown to be integrated with the main business districts of cities and towns? Would Black suppliers have become a part of the mainstream to all business vice Black businesses only? You see, it is impossible to be in the thick of a race when you are repeatedly moved back and everyone else keeps running (progressing). You can run hard to catch up; however, they are not slowing down. That's the story of Blacks in business and economics. It started in 1619. Suppose Blacks from Africa migrated to the United States as did the Europeans and other nationalities. Not only were they brought with nothing, but the system was set up to insure they gained nothing. In fact, the system worked to take away those intangibles that they brought (language, culture, identity). The second set back in the race was 1712 with the Willie Lynch Letter. The third round of setbacks was after the Civil War (the era of Reconstruction) – 1870s – 1900. The fourth was the 1920s -1930s. The fifth was the era 1947 – 1957. The sixth was 1963 – 1974. The seventh is now 2008 – 2020. So, can you stay competitive in the race when you are on your seventh setback and the system is holding fast to insure future setbacks?

The society has rejected the idea of "Affirmative Action." However, without it, equity in employment opportunities and moving up the corporate ladder will never happen. This matter is like a marathon race. When the race (26 miles) starts, blacks are held back until the other runners are 10 to 15 miles into the race. Then when blacks are given the signal to begin the race, obstacles are put in the path to retard their progress (e.g., the Fair Housing Act of the 1968 being ignored for years and then repealed in 1974). There are similar examples in education, health care, employment, etc. For the majority of blacks, the best scenario is simply finishing the race and never placing for a medal. That equates to having a little money in the bank, being able to pay all the bills, and having enough insurance and funds for the funeral.

As pointed out by Armstrong Williams in his Newsmax article, *Why Many Blacks Lag Behind,* dated 11 December 2012, "The economic progress of black America has stalled or declined in the past 20 years." Although Williams' article takes the thesis that much of this is the fault of Blacks, the fact remains that the decline has and is taking place. I will say that although some of the fault may lie with Blacks, the preponderance of the cause lies in the systemic racism, laws and policies of the country, corporate America, government, and culture. As an example, a black owned business oftentimes has to depend on Black clientele for its support. Several factors come into play in that scenario: 1) the clientele are not of financial status such that they can provide the support needed for the business to prosper; 2) more often than not, the black business owner does not have the connections with suppliers that is often enjoyed by white business owners; and 3) the Black business owners hardly ever have the financial capital or investors to open the business in the more lucrative business districts nor open at the level that is most attractive to the consumer – in appearance of the business or cost of the product.

Another major contributor to this economic equation is education. In the 21st century, the need to go to college is being challenged. The push to go to college is being replaced by – 'you can make a great living by getting a trade and you won't have those educational loans to be repaid when you start working' or 'college is not for everyone, you can do just as well by learning a trade'. There are many shortcomings to those philosophies. The major one is how one limits the level of advancement he/she can acquire in the corporation. The second major shortcoming is with a trade in the world of technology one has to be re-trained, when new equipment is acquired, in order to maintain the position currently held. At the same time, they don't have the managerial skills (education) to move up. Some intangibles that exist are the various relationships that exist in the workplace. Blacks generally do not have a relative or close family friend in upper-level management to ensure their retention when changes take place within the company or business. Therefore, their advancement and retention are, to a much greater degree than whites, solely dependent on their performance. Instead of decreasing the push to get a college degree, the black community MUST push for getting a college degree.

The economic picture can only change with a change in the current practices of training for movement up the corporate ladder – making decisive programs to reverse the current trend and give blacks the head start in the race until there is equity.

STEPS TO ECONOMIC EQUALITY

1) Education and acknowledgment by "White America" of the atrocities committed to Native Americans and Black Americans from 1492 to 2020.

2) Establish and execute a massive restitution to both – Native Americans and Black Americans (financial, education, business, etc.)

3) Put into place Affirmative Action to establish equity in all aspects of American life.

As you can see, the probability (likelihood) of the execution of ANY of the three actions listed above is infinitely close to zero. Does this mean we will never reach equality in this country? The short answer is no, it doesn't. However, it does mean that without some divine change in this country, equality will not only NEVER be reached – equality will not be addressed to a level to make any significant difference in the direction of improvement.

TWENTY-THIRD LETTER
A CALL TO SHARE

SYSTEMIC RACISM:

THE CHURCH AND THE STATE

The interval between the dispatch of the twenty-second letter and the initiation of the twenty-third letter has witnessed some historical events. This period has witnessed the continuous denial of defeat by the outgoing US President which has caused havoc with the transfer of leadership. A second major occurrence during this period was the runoff election of two US Senators from the same state. The significance of that event lies in the transfer of power for the US Senate from the Republican Party to the Democratic Party. The third major event, which is somewhat connected to the first event with the outgoing President, was the terrorist attack on the US Capitol.

The above events are referenced during the lead into the discussion of "Religion and the Church," because the events are all directly connected. The period 2015 through 2020 was a period of revelation to recognize how much the church is embedded in US politics. Contrary to the pronouncement of separation of church and state, the last five years have revealed that the church and state are intimately interwoven. Beginning in June 2015 when President Trump announced his candidacy, the evidence began surfacing to show the connection between church and state.

There is not a separation of church and state, rather there is a separation within the church. The church here refers to a body of believers — not the church building. From the beginning of the United States, there has been a separation of church. There is the separation of denominations – even those that profess to believe in the same deity. The separation of church by ethnicity ensures that groups will NEVER accept each other as EQUALS.

`First, to demonstrate the deeply rooted connection of church and state, let's take a look at the abortion issue. The evangelical pro-life stance is rooted in religious belief. The National Review article, *The History of American Evangelics' Opposition to Abortion is Long*, September 10, 2020, by Joseph S. Laughon states, "The true Evangelical history of pro-life advocacy picks up in the early 19th century just as the identity of American Evangelicals was becoming distinct from their Puritan and Presbyterian roots. Olasky notes that, owing to urbanization and industrialization, abortion slowly became more common in the United States.

In response, an alliance of Evangelical doctors, journalists, and reformers pressed for harsher laws to combat what they saw as sinful violence stemming from even more sinful exploitation in the form of prostitution and male abandonment." Note that the avenue utilized early on was governmental laws.

A quick review of Thomas Jefferson's letter to the Danbury Newspaper shows that the original intent of the separation of church and state was to prevent just what the abortion issue has developed into. Jefferson wrote: "Believing with you that religion is a matter which lies solely between Man & his God, that he owes account to none other for his faith or his worship, that the legitimate powers of government reach actions only, & not opinions, I contemplate with sovereign reverence that act of the whole American people which declared that their legislature should 'make no law respecting an establishment of religion, or prohibiting the free exercise thereof,' thus building a wall of separation between Church and State." Jefferson's letter on separation of church and state addresses the state not being in those matters which "lie solely between Man and his God." In many cases the church has pressed to do just the opposite. When the church has an issue it cannot control (i.e., abortion), it turns to government to impose laws. Such is the case with the Roe vs Wade Supreme Court Decision of 1973. However, the Supreme Court did not rule as the church wished. Since that time the church has become increasingly involved with government to get officials elected who support the church's position on issues and Roe vs Wade, although a major issue is not the only one.

In the US Presidential Election in 2016, the "Evangelical Christians" overwhelmingly supported Donald Trump in part because of his position on abortion. The irony is that Donald Trump and the "Evangelical Christians" opposed abortion for very different reasons. Trump became a "pro-life" convert a few years prior to 2011. Before that time, he was a vocal advocate for pro-choice. In a 1999 interview on *NBC Meet the Press*, Trump stated, "Well, look, I'm very pro-choice," Trump said when asked if he would ban partial-birth abortions as president. "I hate the concept of abortion. I hate it. I hate everything it stands for. I cringe when I listen to people debating the subject. But you still – I just believe in choice." So, that was Trump's position until he shared in an interview on CBN in 2011, "One thing about me, I'm a very honorable guy. I'm pro-life, but I changed my view a number of years ago. One of the primary reasons I changed [was] a friend of mine's wife was pregnant, and he didn't really want the baby. He was crying as he was telling me the story," Trump said. "He ends up having the baby and the baby is the apple of his eye. It's the greatest thing that's ever happened to him. And you know here's a baby that wasn't going to be let into life. And I heard this, and some other stories, and I am pro-life." We can see the reason for Trump's position on abortion. It has nothing to do with his religious belief. Although there is a proclaimed separation of church and state, the reality is that laws and bills are often the results of beliefs by a group of people.

On the other hand, the separation of churches is very real and very obvious. Denominations claiming to believe in the same God are physically separated in their respective houses of worship. Within the group called Baptist, there are more than 50 separate groupings within the United States. Within the group called Methodist, there are more than 25 separate groupings within the United States. For both the Baptist and Methodist, the groups in each are totally separated in their worship and governance.

As it affects racism in America, ABC News in a report: *Segregated Sundays: Taking on Race and Religion*, by Dan Harris and Blair Soden, January 21, 2008, "40 years after King's (Martin Luther King, Jr.) murder, only 7 percent of America's churches are considered racially mixed." This was in response to Dr. King's statement in 1963 at Western Michigan University when he said, "At 11:00 on Sunday morning when we stand and sing, and Christ has no east or west, we stand at the most segregated hour in this nation." A Gallup Pole survey in 2002 reported the following findings: "Seventy-three percent of whites, according to this audit, attended mostly white or all-white churches, while 7% attended churches that were approximately half white and half black. Virtually no whites attended churches that were mostly or all black. Among blacks, 71% attended mostly or all-black churches, while 13% attended churches that were equally black and white, and 6% went to churches that were mostly or all white."

The question may be, why is worshiping together such a big issue? Let's begin with the saying, "The family that prays together, stays together." In the Institute for Family Studies April 20, 2016 article, *Does the Family That Prays Together Really Stay Together?* by Ashley McGuire, she reports, "A lot of research has been devoted to the question of whether religion is a force for good among today's families, and while the findings are mixed, studies have found plenty of reason to believe that faith can be a powerful adhesive for families working hard not to come undone." McGuire's article went on to say, "That individual prayer can improve the lives of those who undertake it is a well-documented fact supported by even the secular, medical world. Its benefits can include reduced stress, increased self-awareness, better communication, and a more empathetic and forgiving attitude towards others. Another study found a positive correlation between increased trust and prayer time between couples. Other sociologists have argued that joint prayer can be a powerful mediation tool that leads couples to be more forgiving. As Mark Butler, a professor of marriage and family therapy at Brigham Young University, put it: 'When people pray (about tensions in their relationship) they are helped to see their part in the problem. They're helped to see what they can do themselves to make a difference. And they are helped to soften. All these things help with conflict resolution.'"

It's hardly a stretch to suggest that those benefits identified for individual prayer would expand to families that then pray together. The same factors that result in benefits for families praying together also benefit those in corporate worship. The time spent praying together in a corporate setting provides a time of sharing, a time of empathizing, a time of relating, a time of building on relationships with one another. It is often a time of getting to know one another on a more personal level than provided in any other environment. It helps people see how much they have in common with one another. This is not at all to imply that corporate prayer is designed to enhance relationships. It's purpose remains to communicate with the supreme being of the group. When fulfilling that purpose together, the group develops a more intimate relationship – a relationship that is more open than in any other setting because the central focus is on a higher power than anyone in the group.

In the publication Desiring God, May 25, 2014 article, *Five Benefits of Corporate Worship,* David Mathis, the Executive Editor, provides these as five of the benefits: 1) awakening, 2) assurance, 3) advance, 4) accepting another's leading, and 5) accentuated joy. On the topic of *awakening*, Mathis states, "Worshiping Jesus together may be the single most important thing we do. It plays an indispensable role in rekindling our spiritual fire, and keeping it burning. Corporate worship brings together God's word, prayer, and fellowship, and so makes for the greatest means of God's ongoing grace in the Christian life." Corporate worship, as it is called, draws the participants together with a basic belief that influences every facet of their lives – individual, family, associates, etc. Worshiping together provides the forum for developing trust in one another and an openness to learn about one another. Corporate worship also causes each person to look closely at their beliefs and moral values – this creates the awakening from within.

We also leverage off the benefit of *accepting another's leading.* In the corporate worship setting, we are less focused on an individual's position in society. Again, Mathis points out, "In private worship, we're in the driver's seat. We decide what passage to read, when to pray, what to pray, how long to linger in Bible reading and meditation, what songs to listen to or sing, what gospel truths to preach to ourselves, and what applications to consider. But in corporate worship, we respond. Others preach and pray and select the songs and choose how long to linger in each element. We're positioned to receive.

It is a wonderful thing in our personal devotions to make such choices, but it is also good for us to practice engaging with God when someone other than ourselves is making the calls. Corporate worship demands that we discipline ourselves to respond, and not only pursue God on our own terms. It is an opportunity to embrace being led, and not always taking the lead."

The fifth benefit is *accentuated joy*. The descriptor Mathis gives follows: "Last, but not least, is the heightened experience of worship in the corporate context. Our own awe is accentuated, our own adoration increased, our own joy doubled when we worship Jesus *together*. The secret of joy in corporate worship is not only self-forgetfulness — or to put it positively, preoccupation with Jesus and his glory — but also the happy awareness that we are not alone in having our souls satisfied in him."

The benefits Mathis described are missed as we continue the 'segregated' worship. These benefits are not only valuable during the worship experience, they carry over into our daily lives. The absence of those benefits leaves a void on the potential of removing racism and racial inequality. As written in The Gospel Project, volume 9, number 2, unit 30, session 2, "Christ's desire for the church is that we be united as one in Him by the gospel, reflecting the oneness of our trinitarian God. As such, we (the church/believers) are to allow for NO divisions to separate us, such as ethnicity, socioeconomics, nationality, language, politics, or secondary doctrinal beliefs, but to celebrate the diversity of God's people." Until there is no physical separation in churches, the unity/oneness will NEVER be achieved.

To have the oneness requires a change on the order of "miracle." It requires that there be no separation in worship by different ethnicity. It requires that agape love exist across different nationalities, different political groups (democrats stop blaming republicans and republicans stop blaming democrats), different socioeconomic classes, and different lifestyles. In 1 John 4:20 it states, "Whoever claims to love God yet hates a brother or sister is a liar." Given that statement, it means that the great preponderance of those professing to love God are liars – meaning they don't really love God. In the political world it appears to be the norm that whatever is not going well is blamed on the other party – the democrats blaming the republicans and the republicans blaming the democrats. The country will never be able to move forward with that mentality. Each party takes the position that the other party cannot do anything right. Joe Scarborough, host on that morning's edition of his MSNBC program, *Morning Joe*, on 6 February 2021, described many members of Congress as "having traded their faith in for politics."

The change will require that Sunday morning at eleven o'clock become the most integrated hour in America instead of the way it is that eleven o'clock on Sunday morning being the most segregated hour in America. The democrats and republicans would have to resolve to work with each other and end the block voting by party. These two gigantic actions would change America. What's the likelihood of either of them happening? The one that has the highest probability is the latter – Democrats and Republicans deciding to work together instead of constantly pointing their fingers at one another. That leaves the church. What is the likelihood that churches will change to have congregations consisting of integration of ethnicity?

The church and state, instead of moving toward separation, in recent years has moved more toward consolidating the influence of one upon the other. This is evidenced with the resurgence of conservatism during the 1980s and the appointment of constitutional conservatives to the Supreme Court. In fact, religious beliefs now seem to drive the appoints of federal court judges at all levels.

As stated earlier, the separation within the church could be the major factor in the influence the church has on the state. The separation within the church perpetuates the differences in the orientation of the differences in beliefs. It is therefore my thesis that the greater the separation within the church the less likely there will be a separation of church and state. Because of the separation within the church (the body of believers), the group is unable to establish a baseline of their belief. For example, the believers agree with the biblical doctrine of feeding the poor. However, because of the separation, the believers are very divided on how this doctrine should be executed. And so, it is with a plethora of biblical doctrinal issues. Unity is the major catalyst to eliminating the divisions.

SOLUTION: ALL CHURCHES OF ALL DENOMINATIONS MOVE TOWARD FULLY INTEGRATED CONGREGATIONS.

ROADBLOCK: CULTURE

TOPIC OF LETTER TWENTY-FOUR: THE CHURCH AND CULTURE

TWENTY- FOURTH LETTER
A CALL TO SHARE

SYSTEMIC RACISM:
THE CHURCH AND CULTURE

Churches are separated by cultural factors while in many cases the profession of faith/beliefs are the same. How can that be? Belief and faith are to be the corner stones for the religion, yet culture appears to override faith and belief. In fact, too often culture is the cornerstone of the religion rather than belief. Culture is so woven into the faith that the participants/believers don't recognize that their worship is more based on culture than belief. Antonia Cirjak, in his ATLAS article May 1, 2020, *How Does Culture Affect Religion,* writes, "The interplay between culture and religion never stops, and the two are continually influencing one another in many ways. One thing that we can quickly start to deconstruct to explain this complicated relationship is a view where cultural phenomena are described as something tangible, if not even material. Religion, on the other hand, is often viewed as something that is 'beyond material,' or, better to say, something that speaks of transcendence. However, as soon as we start defining the always escaping notion of the term 'culture' we can see how religious questions are embedded into this concept."

Ashish Daleia in her article, *How Culture Influences Religion*, March 4, 2017, shared the following, "We generally think of religion as something that pertains to *transcendence* beyond the current material existence. The reality, however, is that the day-to-day practice of religion involves societies whose cultural norms must be compatible with the tenets of the religion. If there is a misfit between culture and religion, then most likely the religion would be changed rather than the culture. This fact has important implications for the understanding of religion, namely, that the vision of transcendence we create is often determined by the vision of material existence we currently want to lead. Similarly, those serious about the long-term viability of religion must pay close attention to its cultural fit."

These and others' thoughts on the inter-connectivity of culture and religion are provided to provoke thoughts of your own on the impact of culture on your religion. One of the more profound statements by Deleia above is, "If there is a misfit between culture and religion, then most likely the religion would be changed rather than the culture." This statement is at the core of my thesis that culture overrides religion. One very obvious example in our history is slavery. Slavery was a cultural concept, yet it took precedence over the Biblical teaching that we are all God's children. The culture took it even further by imposing these concepts into Biblical teaching. Examples of the culture influencing religious beliefs include the following:

1) The use of the Bible story of Noah and his sons - Shem, Ham, and Japheth – by "proclaimed Christians" to justify slavery in the United States. Slaves were not brought to America to fulfill a prophesy of God. Slaves were brought to America to provide the free labor and the only way to get free labor was through enslavement. (Time, *How Christian Slaveholders Used the Bible to Justify Slavery*, by Noel Rae Article, 23 February 2018)

2) When Jesus tells the woman at the well in John 4, that she had 5 husbands and the man she has now is not her own, those of us in the western world quickly judge her as a loose woman jumping from man to man. However, in the Eastern world at that time, a woman could not divorce her husband. That means that 5 men had already left her and the man she was with now was not even claiming her. Jesus' message was not that she was a slut. His message was that while everyone else had left her thirsting for love, Jesus, the Living Water, would quench her thirst for

love for all eternity, as He would never leave her. (Posted on the Sabbath School Net, Cultural Influence and the Bible, May 7, 2020 by William Earnhardt)

3) Another example is in Numbers 12, when Miriam and Aaron complain about Moses' Ethiopian wife. Many in the western world think they looked down on her because she was black. That's because we live in a culture that not even 200 years ago had black slaves. But remember that was not the case at the time of Moses' day in the eastern world. The Ethiopians were not slaves. It was the Hebrews that had just been freed from slavery. Instead of looking down on her, they were probably jealous, and were insinuating that Moses thought he was all that, because he upgraded in their minds to an Ethiopian woman. (Posted on the Sabbath School Net, Cultural Influence and the Bible, May 7, 2020 by William Earnhardt)

4) According to segregationist readings of the Bible, black people were inferior to white people, cursed by God and naturally suited to manual labor. Requiring white employers to hire black people would violate these sincerely held religious convictions and threatened once again to destroy the settled racial order of the nation.

The successes of the civil rights movement made overt racial discrimination no longer tenable even under the cover of religious freedom. But although it was forced underground, racial bigotry remained very much alive in the Christianity of white America. (The Washington Post, *Discriminating in the name of religion? Segregationists and slaveholders did it, too*, by Tisa Wenger, associate professor of American religious history at Yale Divinity School, December 5, 2017)

These examples lead to an interesting concept – cultural Christian. So, what is a cultural Christian as opposed to being a Biblical Christian? I will only provide definitions for categories of cultural Christians and a Biblical Christian. Each person needs to do a self-assessment to determine the category into which she/he falls. The definitions are provided by CHRISMANEWS, *Are You a Cultural Christian or a Biblical Christian?*, by Patrick Morley, September 25, 2014.

1) Cultural Christianity means pursuing the God we want instead of the God who is. It is sensing a need for God, but on our own terms. It is wanting the God we have underlined in our Bibles without wanting the rest of Him too. It is God relative instead of God absolute.

2) A Biblical Christian is a person who trusts in Christ, and Christ alone, for his salvation. As a *result* of his saving faith, he desires to be obedient to God's principles out of the overflow of a grateful heart.

Before we jump on the bandwagon proclaiming to be a Biblical Christian, here are some practical considerations. Some would admit that it is more difficult being a Biblical Christian today than it was in earlier generations. In those days the temptations were not so great – there was no explicit sex on television, the music was much more wholesome (for the most part), drugs had not invaded the culture. Those were the obvious ones we often refer too; however, if we look closer, we will see that the greed for money, women and power have been around going back for centuries. And many seeking those things also professed to be Christians. Many will say, I don't partake in any of those things mentioned above. Well, before declaring that I am a Biblical Christian on those bases, let's also consider some other Biblical principals: 1) love thy neighbor as thy self, 2) care for the poor, the hungry, and the downtrodden. Do I live extravagantly while others are suffering? Extravagant living includes – but is not limited to – do I live in a million-dollar home when a $350 thousand home would meet all my needs? The same theory applies if I live in a $350 thousand home when a $200 thousand home would meet my needs. This principal also applies to cars, clothes, entertainment, food, etc.

The material things are among the first that come to mind when we talk about being "my bothers' keeper." However, there are some intangibles that also fall into that category of making me a Cultural Christian. Discriminatory practices fall in that category. Other intangibles include not standing up in situations where people are not being treated right. Recall how Nicodemus and Joseph of Arimathea took a stand when it wasn't popular. On the other side were believers who stood by and said nothing. For the majority group, how often do we stand by and do nothing about unfair employment practices, or unfair treatment, or unjust laws, or laws that take away persons ability to vote, or unfair housing practices? This list goes on and on. By the way, there is no community that is exempt from all of the discriminatory practices listed above. So maybe the question is not, am I a Cultural Christian or a Biblical Christian, but rather what am I doing or not doing that has placed me in the category of Cultural Christian?

The title Cultural Christian, in fact, may fit most of us to some degree. During this time in which we live – the 20th and 21st centuries – there are many events in our culture that challenge our Christianity. As an example, one might claim to be a Biblical Christian yet supports denying citizens the right to vote. What constitutes denial? A major form of denial is invoking requirements that a segment of the population is challenged to meet. Some take it for granted that transportation is available to all. There are many who don't have transportation readily available. To deny them the opportunity to vote via absentee ballots is denying them their right to vote. This is another form of denial which parallels the 1940s and 50s when some segments of the population were required to recite from various federal documents in order to register to vote. Mind you that same segment of the population had previously been denied an education. This is a catch-22 cycle. The same thing applies when we deny a person who has served time incarcerated the right to vote. This list goes on and on. The bottom line is the culture is infested with practices that lead to being a Cultural Christian rather than a Biblical Christian.

Support of a few biblical principals and being non-supportive or in opposition to other biblical principals does not make one a Biblical Christian. In fact, that is the profile of most Cultural Christians. The High Priest and the Religious Council during Jesus' era would have claimed to be Biblical; however, Jesus repeatedly showed them the error of their ways. The early settlers in America who came for religious freedom would likely claim to be Biblical. Yet they disenfranchised the Native Americans and called them savages. Some Americans take the position that if an immigrant wants to live in the United States, they MUST learn and communicate using English. Well, to adhere to that line of thought, all the non-Native Americans (those whose ancestors migrated to America) should advocate for all to learn and speak in the tongues of Native Americans (e.g., speak Navajo, Cherokee, or Apache, etc.).

Stephen Lloyd, PhD Candidate, Graduate Division of Religious Studies, Boston University School of Theology, February 2021 Essay, *Christianity and the World of Cultures* wrote, "Those Christians who embrace surrounding cultures use indigenous language, music, art forms, and rituals as potent resources for their own ends. Christians have a history of taking that which is not Christian, and then filling it with Christian meaning. There are classic examples of this: Christians inherited Roman vestments and German Christmas trees. Yet even at a more basic level, Christians borrow pre-Christian languages and use them for Christian ends. Jesus did not speak Greek, Latin, or English, yet each of those languages has been used to tell his story and teach his message. As Christianity continues to find a home in new cultural settings, Christians continue to borrow new languages and cultures to tell the story of Jesus. In today's world, the questions of gender and sexuality fuel debates among Christians across cultural lines. As Christians become increasingly aware of their cultural differences, the study of World Christianity will provide tools for navigating the diversity."

As for the White church, I am not sure that the needle has moved very far from the comments made by Frederick Douglass. From his book, Narrative of the Life of Frederick Douglass by Frederick Douglass, first published in 1845, he had this to say: "Between the Christianity of this land and the Christianity of Christ, I recognize the widest possible difference—so wide that to receive the one as good, pure, and holy, is of necessity to reject the other as bad, corrupt, and wicked. To be the friend of the one is of necessity to be the enemy of the other. I love the pure, peaceable, and impartial Christianity of Christ; I therefore hate the corrupt, slaveholding, women-whipping, cradle-plundering, partial and hypocritical Christianity of this land. Indeed, I can see no reason but the most deceitful one for calling the religion of this land Christianity…"

There appears to be a ground swell within the "Christian" community citing the need for a "Great Revival." A brief historical review of great revivals will set the stage for what we are seeking in the form of a "Great Revival" in the 21st Century. The CHURCHLEADERS Newsletter, printed an article, *A Brief History of Spiritual Revival and Awakening in America,* by Patrick Morley, June 4, 2019, providing a chronology of Great Revivals. He wrote, "Great Awakening, 1734-43. In December 1734, the first revival of historic significance broke out in Northampton, Massachusetts, where a young Jonathan Edwards was pastor. Three hundred souls converted in six months—in a town of only 1,100 people! The news spread like wildfire, and similar revivals broke out in over 100 towns.

Second Great Awakening, 1800-1840. In 1800, only one in 15 of America's population of 5,300,000 belonged to an evangelical church. Presbyterian minister James McGready presided over strange spiritual manifestations in Logan County, Kentucky. The resulting camp meeting revivals drew thousands from as far away as Ohio. Rev. Gardiner Spring reported that for the next 25 years not a single month passed without news of a revival somewhere. In 1824, Charles Finney began a career that would eventually convert 500,000 to Christ. An unparalleled 100,000 were converted in Rochester, N.Y., in 1831 alone – causing the revival to spread to 1,500 towns. By 1850, the nation's population exploded fourfold to 23,000,000 people, but those connected to evangelical churches grew nearly tenfold from seven percent to 13 percent of the population—from 350,000 to 3,000,000 church members!

The Businessmen's Revival of 1857-1858. In 1857, the North Dutch Church in New York City hired a businessman, Jeremiah Lanphier, to be a lay missionary. He prayed, "Lord, what would you have me do?" Concerned by the anxious faces of businessmen on the streets of New York City, Lanphier decided to open the church at noon so businessmen could pray. The Great Prayer Meeting Revival, an estimated 1,000,000 people were added to America's church rolls, and as many as 1,000,000 of the 4,000,000 existing church members also converted.

Revivals of 1905-1906. Word of the Welsh Revival of 1904-1905 spread to Welsh-speaking settlers in Pennsylvania in late 1904 and revival broke out. By 1905, local revivals blazed in places like Brooklyn, Michigan, Denver, Schenectady, Nebraska, North and South Carolina, Georgia, Taylor University, Yale University, and Asbury College in Wilmore, Kentucky. Billy Sunday, who became a key figure about this time, preached to more than 100,000,000 people with an estimated 1,000,000 or more conversions.

xcEach revival or awakening leaves its own heat signature; in 1740 youth led the way, in 1857 businessmen and prayer took center stage, and the 1906 Azusa Street revival was decidedly interracial.

A majority of Americans believe our country is going downhill. Yet church attendance as a percent of population has held steady since 1990, and probably since 1940. America added 50,000 new churches in the last 20 years of the 20th century to total 350,000. The number of born-again Christians has grown steadily to 46 percent of adults today. Given the state of moral and spiritual decay, how is that possible? The answer is simple. Today, Christianity is prevalent, but not powerful. The solution is spiritual revival and awakening."

Before a revival, we must recognize and acknowledge the state of the church today – both the Black church and the white church. Here are some of the potential arguments against integrated church congregations: 1) preaching styles, 2) music, 3) differing views on interracial dating, 4) the appropriate racial mix of church leaders. As for the Black church, some of the thoughts may parallel these that follow: "The black church is our best institution," says Michael Reel, co-editor for reelurbannews.com and former managing editor of the Baptist Voice. "It's ours – it's the one last place in the world that we can call our own." Reel says many African Americans are changing from historically black churches to religious houses that are predominantly white.

But Pastor Bobby T. Newman of Citizens of Zion Missionary Baptist Church in Compton, California, says "black churches can't afford to lose members to other churches." Newman said, "It creates a great burden on the church financially and leaves a void for younger African Americans culturally."

As pointed out above, the prevailing request for revival is valid. Note that the last of the great revivals (1906) was largely interracial. The implication is – given a great revival in the 21st century – what should we expect? With the current activities of racial disparity, racism, gender biases (LGBTQ is an acronym for lesbian, gay, bisexual, transgender, and queer or questioning), ethnic disparities, and others, I submit that a revival in the 21st century would include all of these categories of people. Is the Black church, the white church, the evangelical church, the Catholic church or any other church ready to accept these categories into their congregations? Just as the last great revival was decidedly interracial (at a time when segregation was a way of life), we should expect a revival of the 21st century to consist of groups/categories different than the make-up of the current congregation. Is the church ready for that? Is that a cultural or biblical question?

STEPS TO MOVE MORE TOWARD BEING BIBLICAL CHRISTIANS:

1. Acknowledge that we are ALL Cultural Christians.

2. Seek to identify those things causing me to fall short of being a Biblical Christian.

3. Humble myself to accept that those things I have believed all my life are keeping me from being Biblical.

4. As we encounter situations requiring Godly actions, stop and think: Are the actions I am considering Biblical or cultural; then follow the Biblical.

5. Convince myself and others that we must CHANGE and fulfill Micah 6:8.

He has shown you, O man, what is good;
And what does the LORD require of you
But to DO JUSTLY,
To LOVE MERCY,
And to WALK HUMBLY with your God?

TWENTY- FIFTH LETTER
A CALL TO SHARE

SYSTEMIC RACISM:

WHY SO MANY WHITE PEOPLE REFUSE TO UNDERSTAND RACISM?

As you look at the topic of this chapter, one thought may be that there are White persons who don't understand racism, but it is not that they refuse to understand. That's a valid thought; however, with the amount of visibility given to the topic each person has the opportunity – if she/he wishes – to learn about racism. In fact, it is difficult to avoid the issue because of the level of press that has been given during the period 2019 and 2021. Thus, although there may be those who don't understand, every responsible citizen has the obligation to understand the issues facing the society in which they live.

Linda Chavers writes in her article, *What too many white people still don't understand about racism*, in the Boston Globe, 6/9/20, "Many white Americans looking at the news over the last few weeks think they are seeing the most inappropriate expressions of personal despair and outrage. They see protests, then riots, then looting, and even well-intentioned white people might think, *That's not the best way to be heard*, as if there is one way to disobey civilly. Some might even feel fear for themselves, or more likely, for their property. After all, the destruction of property gets more time on the news than speakers voicing righteous anger at the violence enacted on Black bodies.

Still, here's the truth: You have not seen outrage until you have seen the face of a white person being called a racist. You would think seeing

ZKE ZIMMERMAN

the image of Emmett Till's mutilated corpse in an open casket in 1955 or Michael Brown's body lying dead in a Missouri street in 2014 would evoke extreme shock and horror. But, actually, white people get the most worked up when they or someone they know have been labeled a racist."

The attitude described by Chavers contributes significantly to the lack of understanding. In fact, it places many on the azimuth of misunderstanding, rather than seeking to understand. One of the more misunderstood and misinterpreted areas in the fight to combat racism is the "Black Lives Matter" campaign. Many label that campaign based on the news media and commentaries which focus on violence and looting. These are in no way the defining bases for the "Black Lives Matter" campaign. Rather than learning about the campaign, the violence and looting scenarios justify disapproval. Thus, contributing to the thesis of refusal to learn about and understand racism.

Next comes the question, 'Why the attitude of looking for justification rather than trying to understand the underlying issues?' The next section is rather extensive in order to capture the full thrust of what the author of that segment is communicating. Jamie Utt, Founder and Director of Education at CivilSchools, in Feminism Magazine article - *Here Are the Real Reasons Why We White People Struggle to Admit That Racism Still Exists*, July 1, 2015, shared reasons why Whites refuse to understand racism: "1)White People Must Choose to Extend Their Personal Values towards Racial Issues, 2) White People Benefit Materially from Racism, 3) White People Have an Emotional Stake in Denying White Supremacy, and 4) Working towards Racial Solidarity Means Being Vulnerable." Utt goes on to explain each of these factors. The first with regard to necessity for White people to extend their personal values towards racial issues, Utt explains, "Racism is about the ways that virtually all of the systems in which we live (economic, educational, judicial, medical, and so on) were created to serve White people (particularly White, cisgender, straight men) while oppressing people of Color. So if we only see racism as flying the Confederate battle flag over a state capitol or as an individual racist gunman, it makes sense that we get so damn defensive when the topic of

152

race and racism comes up. 'Few of us want to be associated with that blatant hate.' But to understand the issues of race and racism that are being tackled by anti-racist movements like #BlackLivesMatter, we White folks need to make sure we're being clear about the difference between Whiteness (also sometimes called White supremacy) and White people. Why was Whiteness created? For social control: to allow wealthy White elites to unite poor and middle-class Whites against people of Color. Whiteness, then, refers to that system of social control and its institutions that were built to serve White wealth and power concentration."

Dr. Robin DiAngelo further explains in her article, *Why It's So Hard to Talk to White People About Racism*, in Huffpost, December 6, 2017, the reluctance/refusal of Whites to understand or talk about racism. She writes, "Any white person living in the United States will develop opinions about race simply by swimming in the water of our culture. But mainstream sources — schools, textbooks, media — don't provide us with the multiple perspectives we need. Yes, we will develop strong emotionally laden opinions, but they will not be informed opinions. Our socialization renders us racially illiterate. When you add a lack of humility to that illiteracy (because we don't know what we don't know), you get the break-down we so often see when trying to engage white people in meaningful conversations about race."

It bears taking a closer look at Utt's stated reasons why Whites struggle to admit racism exists. The first of the stated reasons is White People Must Choose to Extend Their Personal Values towards Racial Issues. The admitting that racism exists would require Whites to revamp their personal values in numerous areas, including: socially, spiritually, economically, educationally, politically, morally, etc. – which involves almost all, if not all, aspects of their lives. To admit racism exists would be admitting that the church has been deficient (failed) in carrying out its role of unifying. To admit that racism exists would be admitting that the political platforms of the political parties are not consistent with the constitution – "of the people, by the people, and for the people." Rather the political systems' platforms are – "by white people and for white people." To admit that racism exists would be admitting that the educational system – its curriculum, funding, policies, etc. – are not equitable for all, rather they are only equitable for middle and upper class whites. To admit that racism exists would be admitting that the economic systems and policies are biased against all non-whites. To admit the systems are biased would require paying proper wages for a large segment of the society. Likewise, it would mean the top two percent of the wealthiest would see a significant decline in wealth accumulation. As the middle and lower classes were standing in food lines, falling behind in their rent/mortgage, car payments and medical care during the pandemic, the billionaires were increasing significantly in their wealth levels. As reported on the Columbia Broadcasting System (CBS) by Aimee Picchi, March 31, 2021 Money Watch, "Between March 18, 2020, and March 18, 2021, the wealth held by the world's 2,365 billionaires jumped from $8.04 trillion to $12.39 trillion, according to the Institute for Policy Studies (IPS) analysis of data from Forbes, Bloomberg and Wealth-X. Amazon.com founder Jeff Bezos, the world's wealthiest person, saw his fortune soar to $178 billion from $113 billion, or 57%, during that time, the study found. All told, the total wealth of the world's billionaire class grew 54% during the pandemic year, IPS reported." Thus, by using the stock exchange as the measuring stick for how the economy was doing during the pandemic, one would get the picture that the economy was doing well. It was doing well for the wealthy, but quite the opposite for everyone other than the wealthy.

Another of Utt's reasons worth noting is 'White People Have an Emotional Stake in Denying White Supremacy'. To admit racism would imply that I – as a white person – would be a White Supremacist. In fact, denying that racism exists- when it actually does – is closer akin to being a White Supremacist. The simplistic definition of White Supremacy limits it to the extreme and overt acts of racism. To underwrite the multitude of societal inequities (institutional racism) is equally damaging as the overt acts – in fact, in many cases the acts of institutional racism have a damaging effect on more people for much longer periods of time than the overt acts of racism.

Debby Irving, a racial justice educator and writer, has provided a detailed and interesting essay on how racism has and is damaging White people – the emotional foundation. In her essay, *How Racism Damages Us as White People,* January 2018 and copyright 2021, and her book, *Waking Up White,* she writes, *"So, how racism harms us as white people…"*

• We live with lies – lies about who we are and how the world works. We are told in implicit and explicit ways, for example, that it is inevitable that some people will be on the bottom. When we look around and see white people in large suburban homes with beautifully manicured lawns and black people living ten minutes away in substandard housing – we are told that there is nothing we can do, that "those people" just need to work harder. We are told that we live in a meritocracy.

• We do not know who we really are. We do not know where the fruit of our own labor ends and where the benefits bestowed upon us by privilege begin. It is impossible to separate those things.

• Our anger so often turns to disdain/contempt/judgment (out of feelings of superiority) really quickly, imperceptibly. Our anger often becomes a tool of domination over others, and this is especially true for us as white men. If I am in a position of power relative to the person/people I am angry at, I expect to be able to rant and rave and have things changed for me. If I am not in a position of power in the particular situation, I suppress my anger and stuff it down, with the result that it comes out sideways at a later time, often at the expense of women or people of color. Our inability to use anger except in conjunction with our unearned privilege limits our ability to use it for creative purposes (as Audre Lorde discusses in "The Uses of Anger").

• The love we give and receive in our closest relationships is tangled up with dehumanization and violence (the passing down of a house and land that was stolen from Native Americans; the giving of diamonds from mines in Liberia or South Africa; a mother or father singing "10 little Indian boys" as a favorite song to their young children).

• We misjudge where danger really is (we fear black men coming into our neighborhoods to rob and steal; we fear black men raping our sisters and daughters, though they are in much more danger from other white men – an uncle who molests, the young man in college who date rapes).

• We misunderstand freedom - thinking that privileges that our world dominance achieves on the backs of others (especially on the backs of people of color both here and abroad) is freedom.

• White supremacy tells us we are superior, we have our stuff together, we have the answers to the world's problems. This illusory sense can leave us totally incapable of sustained work to dismantle racism, where we don't have the answers, can't solve the problems alone, and lack the ongoing awareness and insight of how racism is impacting people of color.

• We lose out on the incredible gifts of people of color:

• Think, for example, of what our country could have become with another 40 years of leadership from Martin and Malcolm, both who were assassinated before they reached 40 years of age, because they challenged white racism and U.S. imperialism.

• Think of the genius denied nurturance during slavery, or that genius, which is languishing now in most of our urban public schools.

• Think of the incredible loss to our world caused by mass incarceration and the ongoing separation of black and brown fathers from their children and communities.

• Think if the Europeans arriving in the Americas had been able to learn from the examples of sustainable living practiced here – because they weren't, we are now playing a leading role in the process of destroying ourselves and the planet.

• The richness of our own ethnic, cultural, and linguistic heritage is literally whitewashed.

• We allow ourselves to be in conflict with other middle, working class, and poor folks, which distracts us from changing a system which exploits us all and funnels money and resources to the wealthy.

• One of the reasons this country did not pass universal health care back during the presidency of Roosevelt is that the American Medical Association lobbied to kill the idea before it gained traction because it would have forced the integration of hospitals in the south. And one of the reasons we didn't pass it this time is the power that the Tea Party movement gained, with much of the emotional force of its power coming from racial fearmongering, as evidenced by the slogan, "We want our country back."

• Most of the structural impediments to voting that continue to disenfranchise millions in this country (for example, the Electoral College system, and the fact that voter registration is not automatic when you get your driver license, but still requires an extra step) — most of those structural impediments are vestiges of explicitly racist policies.

• This country's current president (Trump) was elected in large part because he harnessed a wave of racist backlash and resentment against Barack Obama as the first black president, and the ongoing advancement of people of color represented by that historic first. It is a racism that explicitly seeks to oppose anything that Obama proposed (first and foremost expanded health care for poor people). And it is a racism that has led to the U.S. taking concrete steps toward endangering life on the planet in two ways: 1) By denying global warming and undermining all efforts to proactively confront climate challenges, including abandoning the Paris Treaty; and 2) by provoking nuclear war with North Korea.

• We learn to remain silent in the presence of injustice; we learn to live with senseless cruelty done to those who are not like us; we put boundaries around our love, and we suffer immensely from being loved in circumscribed ways; we have a difficult time accepting and loving all of who we are, and we have a difficult time loving others as well; we want to pledge unconditional love to our children, but they see that there *are* conditions to our love, for they see us remain silent in the face of others' pain, and love could not be so silent, love could not give up or give in so easily. Our children feel the lie, as we felt the lie — there are parts of us that were not loved. (Not that doing anti-racism work makes us suddenly able to love perfectly and unconditionally; we are imperfect in our humanity, we are at once whole and broken; but racism takes those breaks, those gaps, those tears, and lengthens and widens and deepens them. Some people are ripped apart completely).

• Racial segregation cuts us off from forming deep and lasting relationships with people of color. In so doing, racism has succeeded in cutting us off from personal connections to those who are being hit by the oppression and violence of racism, and those relationships are what would most naturally pull us into the anti-racist work we need to be doing for our own liberation, for the restoration of our own souls."

The Washington monthly published an article, *What White America Still Doesn't Understand About Racism: A new survey finds a yawning gap between black and white perceptions about slavery's lasting impacts.* By Anne Kim, November 23, 2019, which captures the major areas of misunderstanding or refusal to understand by whites on racism. She writes, "In 2016, the median white household held roughly ten times the net wealth of the median black household; the average black worker earned 73 cents on the dollar compared to his or her white colleagues; and even among college graduates, blacks earned 20 percent less than their white counterparts. For decades, racial disparities in wealth and wages have been stark and enduring – and frustratingly impervious to change.

To many liberals, these inequities are the obvious legacy of slavery and decades of legalized discrimination, such as under Jim Crow. The substandard education to which black Americans have been relegated has meant fewer students succeed in school and in the workforce. Segregated housing, too, has left many people living in neighborhoods without access to good jobs, reliable public transportation, or quality health care. These systematic inequalities are among the many destructive by-products of "structural" racism."

Thus, we have a multiplicity of factors when it comes to answering the question, WHY SO MANY WHITES REFUSE TO UNDERSTAND RACISM? Not all the factors apply to one person or one situation; however, to every person or situation there are several factors which do apply. The challenge is for each person to look DEEP in the mirror and identify those factors which apply to her or him. The first step in this process is to admit – I DON'T UNDERSTAND RACISM AND

I WILL BE OPEN TO LEARNING ABOUT IT. It is written that there are times you should "lean not on your own understanding." If I am one of those who thinks that racism does not exist and that it is not one of the major variables in practically all aspects of the American culture, then I need to go to the mirror.

If two men are competing in a race,
and the second person is required to go back to the starting line
each time he gets within five yards of catching the first person,
what are the chances that the second person
will ever catch up to the first person or
that the second person will win the race?

When you answer that question,
you have answered the question
"Is racism prevalent in America?"